TONGUES

IN

BIBLICAL

PERSPECTIVE

Tongues
in
Biblical
Perspective

A Summary of
Biblical Conclusions
Concerning Tongues

By Charles R. Smith, Th.D.

Professor of Greek and Theology
Grace Theological Seminary
Winona Lake, Indiana

Published by
BMH BOOKS
Winona Lake, Indiana 46590

To

my

wife

Ellie

and our sons

Stephen and Douglas

who make every endeavor

more meaningful.

First Printing, August 1972
Second Printing, September 1973
    (Revised Edition)
Third Printing, October 1976

Foreword

In more than a decade of teaching the Word of God on both the college and graduate level, Dr. Charles R. Smith has demonstrated his skill in handling the Scriptures in the original languages. In recent years, as one of my faithful colleagues in the Department of Theology at Grace Theological Seminary, Dr. Smith has been of great help to me personally in understanding the Biblical doctrine of tongues. His years of studying the modern tongues movement in the light of Scripture finally culminated in a superb 500-page doctoral dissertation, which has been condensed and popularized in the present work.

I am happy to commend this study to the Christian world. In a uniquely clear and concise fashion, Dr. Smith has pointed the searchlight of Scripture to the major problems that surround the phenomenon of tongues. In my opinion, his contribution is especially noteworthy on: (1) the purpose of tongues in New Testament times; (2) the nature of tongues in Acts and 1 Corinthians; (3) the duration of tongues in the light of Mark 16 and 1 Corinthians 13; and (4) the psychological factors involved in the modern tongues movement. In these areas especially, and in others as well, Dr. Smith has brought to light vitally important information that I have not seen elsewhere so clearly presented.

Christians today find it more necessary than ever before to "try the spirits to see whether they be of God" (1 John 4:1). Dr. Smith has set before all of us a worthy example of how to "prove all things" against the infallible measuring stick of Holy Scripture. May God help His church today to do just that!

John C. Whitcomb
Professor of Theology and Old Testament
Grace Theological Seminary

Table of Contents

Introduction

It is certainly an understatement to say that there is no unanimity of opinion among evangelical Christians relative to the various aspects of the tongues issue. A great deal of this confusion results from a tendency to base conclusions on personal relationships, personalities, and experiences. This tendency is not limited to those who favor tongues speaking today, but is also characteristic of most of its opponents. It is difficult to overcome one's preconceptions.

If tongues were not a part of one's personal experience or the experience of those from whom he received his religious heritage, he may easily conclude that they are not a legitimate spiritual gift for today. The usual justification for such a conclusion is to assert that Biblical tongues were clearly miraculous, and since it can be easily demonstrated that modern tongues require no miracles, the modern phenomena is to be adjudged on this basis as illegitimate. Another approach is to argue that Biblical tongues had a unique purpose among Jews only and therefore are not to be experienced among Gentiles today.

On the other side of the issue, many people point out that dear, sincere Christian friends speak in tongues; and surely, it is asserted, when such people have sought a spiritual gift, God would not allow them to be deceived by an experience which is not genuine. Others affirm that where believers are as spiritually minded as was the early church, all the gifts and powers seen then will appear today.

Actually, none of the preceding arguments have Biblical validity. They are all rationalizations for the purpose of supporting one's preconceptions. Far too often they only serve to justify the opinions one holds as a result of the personalities and experiences to which he has been exposed. This approach is to be avoided at all cost. Personalities and experiences are subject to varied interpretations. Evangelical Christianity has long held that the *Scriptures* are the sole rule of faith and practice. Some would respond that the Scriptures also are subject to diverse interpretations. The difference, however, is that the Scriptures are *God's* recorded revelation—and they include revelation on this subject. This revelation is recorded in *words* and these words are subject to lexical and grammatical analysis. If allowed to speak for itself, this revelation can provide a framework within which experiences may be correctly evaluated. The proper approach is to explain experiences within the framework of the Biblical revelation, and not to explain the Biblical revelation within the framework of experiences.

A study of this subject should not be approached lightly. Even in Paul's day some had already closed their minds on this issue. They felt they already had all the answers (1 Cor. 14:36-37). No amount of divine revelation or careful exegesis will affect the opinions of such people. That is why the apostle solemnly adds at the end of his discussion of tongues, "But if any man be ignorant, let him be ignorant" (1 Cor. 14:38). Argumentation and analysis will be to no avail unless one is willing to accept what the Scriptures say even when they contradict his preconceptions.

It is the author's prayer that those who read this book will read it *prayerfully* as they examine the Scriptures in determining whether these things are so (Acts 17:11). *This book should be read only with an open Bible, an open heart, and an open mind*—the heart and mind open to the entrance of His Word, which gives light (Ps. 119:130).[1]

---

[1]When Biblical quotations are not from the Authorized Version (King James), or otherwise designated, they are the author's translations.

6

CHAPTER 1

The Place of Tongues in History

Pre-Christian Tongues

Most people assume that tongues speaking first oc-curred on the Day of Pentecost. The evidence is clear, though, that there were many instances of such utter-ances previous to the Pentecostal experience.

Theologians and psychiatrists use the technical term "glossolalia" for the utterances of those who speak in tongues. Since it is foreign to the ear of most laymen, the author will avoid using this word, though it will occur in a few quotations. It should be understood as synonymous with the word "tongues."

Possible Old Testament references to tongues

There are no clear references to tongues in the Old Testament, but many who have studied the subject have concluded that there are intimations that such phenom-ena occurred.

This opinion is generally based upon the usage of the Hebrew words for "prophet" *(nābî̂)* and "prophesy" *(nāba')*. Lexicons have generally stated that these words come from a root meaning "TO CAUSE TO BUBBLE

UP, hence *to pour forth* words *abundantly,* as is done by those who speak with ardour or divine emotion of mind" (Gesenius, p. 525). Recently some scholars have suggested that the basic idea suggests a divine *call.* In either case the emphasis is on the fact that "inspired" and thus not normal speech was involved. The verb form was used to designate the speech of any person considered to be possessed by any supposedly supernatural power, or any speaking as a result of such an experience. This is why the word could be used even of pagan prophets to indicate ecstatic behavior and was not limited to the designation of a declaration of a divine revelation.

The prophets of Baal were "prophesying" during their fatal contest with Elijah (1 Kings 18:29). Because the word designates either ecstatic or supposedly inspired utterance, it is often translated by forms of the verb "to rave." Lexicons list as one meaning of the verb "to act as if mad," or "raving" (Gesenius, p. 526). Those who had an ecstatic experience often would claim inspiration and demand respect as a prophet. In the Book of Jeremiah, Shemaiah speaks of "every man that is *mad,* and maketh himself a prophet" (Jer. 29:26). The young prophet who came before Jehu at the moment of his revolt was called a *"mad* fellow" (2 Kings 9:11).

Certainly Saul had some type of ecstatic experience on the occasions when he met with the bands of prophets. In the first instance as he was prophesying his behavior was so striking that it could be said that he was "turned into another man" (1 Sam. 10:6). On a later occasion while he prophesied he stripped off his clothes and lay naked on the ground for a day and a night (1 Sam. 19:24). It is also striking that it was while he was prophesying (many versions translate "raved") that he took up his spear and attempted to kill David (1 Sam. 18:10-11).

Obviously, the word "prophesy" is not limited to a

declaration of divine truths. It may refer to any type of unusual, ecstatic, or supposedly "inspired" speech. Thus, while there is no *explicit* reference to tongues speaking in the Old Testament, there are several accounts about unusual utterances which could well have included it (see Num. 11:26-29). With the broad range of meaning of the word "prophesy," it is easy to understand how Joel's prediction of prophesying as a result of the Spirit's work could have covered the tongues at Pentecost (Joel 2:28; Acts 2:17-18; notice Peter's repetition of the word "prophesy").

Extrabiblical references

Extrabiblical records are quite explicit with regard to unintelligible ecstatic utterances prior to the Christian era. As early as 1100 B.C. an Egyptian, Wen-Amon, recorded an incident when a young man in Canaan, seemingly "inspired" by his god, behaved strangely and spoke ecstatically all one night (Pritchard, pp. 25-29).

In three of Plato's dialogues he makes references to religious ecstatic speech. He discusses prophetic "madness" as a departure from one's normal senses. He cites the utterances of the prophetess at Delphi, the priestess at Dodona, and the Sibyl as examples of such madness or ecstasy. Only when those women were "out of their senses," that is, when their speech was unintelligible, were their utterances considered significant. He also describes the incomprehensible speech of certain diviners whose utterances were expounded by an attendant prophet or interpreter (Hutchins, vol. 7).

In the *Aeneid* Virgil describes the sibylline priestess on the island of Delos who, in an ecstatic state, spoke obscurely and unintelligibly. Such utterances were considered the result of some type of divine inspiration, and when "interpreted" by a priest or prophet they were considered divine oracles (Hutchins, vol. 13, bk. 6).

It is apparent that tongues speaking occurred in pagan cultures prior to the day of Pentecost. Martin concludes that tongues have appeared in varying circumstances, among different peoples, and in various periods of history. They have even appeared "outside the area of strictly religious phenomenon," and therefore "no claim may be made for glossolalia as an exclusively Christian demonstration" (Martin, p. 13).

Christian Tongues Speaking

New Testament occurrences

Speaking in tongues is mentioned in only a few New Testament passages (Mk. 16:17; Acts 2:1-13; 8:14-17, by inference; 10:44-48 with 11:15-17; 19:1-7; 1 Cor. 12–14). The New Testament contains no reference to any tongues experience later than the contemporaneous occurrences at Ephesus (Acts 19) and Corinth in A.D. 55.

Occurrences prior to 1900

It will not be possible to examine every claimed reference to tongues speaking during this period, therefore reports of isolated or individual tongues utterances will not be enumerated. All the *groups* or *movements,* however, in which tongues played a significant part are here briefly reviewed. Those who desire further information on these groups may find it in the works by Martin, Cutten, Mackie, and Hayes which are listed in the bibliography.

Montanists.—In the second century a Phrygian named Montanus became noted for his heresies concerning the Holy Spirit and for the prediction of his coming kingship over the New Jerusalem, which he expected to descend to

Phrygia during his lifetime. His contemporaries stated clearly that he and his attendant prophetesses entered ecstatic states and spoke unintelligibly. References to the Montanists are the only authentic accounts about any group of tongues speakers between the Apostolic Age and the Reformation.

Cevenol Prophets.—Tongues played no part in the Reformation movement. Following the revocation of the Edict of Nantes in 1685 the "gift of prophecy" and ecstatic phenomena occurred among the persecuted Protestants in southern France. It was said that even very young children who knew only the local dialect spoke in perfect French while in a trance. The group was soon discredited because of their night raids and military reprisals against their enemies and because their prophecies went unfulfilled.

Jansenists.—A group of Roman Catholic reformers, the Jansenists were opposed to the new doctrines of the Reformation, yet also opposed to the Jesuits and persecuted by them. About the year 1731 they held night meetings at a former leader's tomb, where reportedly ecstatic phenomena, including tongues, occurred. One Pentecostal writer has stated that this group of Roman Catholics was the first sect in modern times to exhibit Pentecostal behavior (Kendrick, p. 20).

Shakers.—"Mother" Ann Lee (1736-1784) regarded herself as the "female principle in Christ" and Jesus as the male principle. In 1776 she founded the Shaker community near Troy, New York. She taught that the second coming of Christ was fulfilled in her. She also received a "revelation" to the effect that sexual intercourse, even within marriage, was the cause of all human corruption. It is said that in order to "mortify" the flesh (!) she instituted the practice of men and women dancing together naked while they spoke in tongues.

Irvingites.—Edward Irving, a Scotch Presbyterian minister, believed that all the apostolic gifts should be evidenced in his day. A young woman, Mary Campbell, in 1830 was the first in this group, later named the Catholic Apostolic Church, to speak in tongues. Others in this London group (notable among them was Robert Baxter) soon demonstrated gifts, also. The "gift of prophecy" was given preeminence. The Irvingites were soon discredited for several reasons. (1) Their "revelations" were frequently contradictory to the Word, and their prophecies were not fulfilled. (2) Baxter later renounced the movement and attributed all his own "gifts" to the work of evil spirits. (3) Mary Campbell confessed that she had been dishonest and had been guilty of calling her own utterances the voice of God. (4) Supposedly miraculous healings were followed by death. (5) There were rumors of immorality.

Mormons.—Right from the beginning with Joseph Smith, Mormons have accepted tongues as a valid gift for modern times. When their temple was dedicated in Salt Lake City, hundreds of elders spoke in tongues. Brigham Young supposedly prayed in the "pure Adamic language" (which unfortunately was not recorded for scholarly evaluation!).

Others.—There were other smaller groups, mostly heretical sects, in which tongues occurred, but there were no other major movements. Reports of tongues at Loudun and at Lourdes in France, for example, because of occult and immoral connections are often attributed even by tongues advocates to demonic activity.

Twentieth Century Tongues

Four factors figure prominently in the development of

the modern tongues movement, or "charismatic revival" as it is called.

The Holiness movement.—In eastern Tennessee and western North Carolina in 1886 a "holiness revival" was begun under the leadership of two Baptist preachers, R. G. Spurling and R. G. Spurling, Jr. In 1902 the "Holiness Church" was formed, and the following year A. J. Tomlinson became its pastor. His efforts led to the establishment of the Church of God. In these early Holiness revivals, tongues and other ecstatic phenomena were not uncommon.

Bethel Bible College.—Charles Parham has been called "the father of the modern Pentecostal movement." He established Bethel Bible College at Topeka, Kansas, in 1900. When he left town in December for a preaching engagement, he assigned his students the task of answering the question, "What is the Bible evidence of the baptism of the Holy Ghost?" They concluded that speaking in tongues was the evidence and began to pray fervently for this experience. On January 1, 1901, student Agnes Ozman "received the baptism." Because this was the first occasion in modern times when this experience followed intense and fervent efforts to receive such a "baptism," this has been called the birthday of Pentecostalism.

Azusa Street.—In 1905 Parham established a Bible school in Houston, Texas. The following year one of his black students, W. J. Seymour, was invited to speak in a small mission church in Los Angeles. Though the church at first rejected him, tongues soon appeared in a prayer meeting. The black group grew rapidly, with whites joining them, so that it became necessary to move to larger quarters. An old building on Azusa Street, later known as the Azusa Street Mission, became the "Mecca" of Pentecostalism. Holiness pastors, especially from the South, flocked to this center. A chain reaction has produced Pentecostal churches with a membership of over two million.

Ecumenicity.—Prior to 1960 tongues speaking, at least outwardly, was almost wholly limited to Pentecostal churches. On April 3, 1960, Father Dennis Bennett, rector of a large Episcopal church in Van Nuys, California, announced to his congregation that he had spoken in tongues. Nationwide publicity followed. This has been acclaimed as the beginning of the "charismatic revival" within the historic, or "mainline," denominations. Since that date numerous other non-Pentecostal churchmen have announced their approval of or participation in tongues speaking. All of the major denominations have been affected, and in recent years the greatest growth in tongues speaking has been seen among Roman Catholics.

Non-Christian Tongues

In non-Christian religions.—Tongues occupied a significant place in ancient Greek religion. The seeress at Delphi, not far from Corinth, spoke in tongues. According to Plutarch (A.D. 44-117), interpreters were kept in attendance to explain her incoherent utterances. Many scholars have stated that tongues were experienced in the mystery religions (Osiris, Mithra, Eleusinian, Dionysian, and Orphic cults). Some have concluded that the unintelligible lists of "words" in the "magical papyri" and in certain Gnostic "prayers" are records of ecstatic utterances. About A.D. 180 Celsus reported ecstatic utterances among the Gnostics. Lucian of Samosata (A.D. 120-198) described tongues speaking as it was practiced by the devotees of the Syrian goddess, Juno.

Today shamans (witch doctors, priests, or medicine

men) in Haiti, Greenland, Micronesia, and countries of Africa, Australia, Asia, and North and South America speak in tongues. Several groups use drugs to aid in inducing the ecstatic state and utterances. Voodoo practitioners speak in tongues. Buddhist and Shinto priests have been heard speaking in tongues. Moslems have spoken in tongues, and an ancient tradition even reports that Mohammed himself spoke in tongues. According to his own account, after his ecstatic experiences he found it difficult to return to "logical and intelligible speech" (Kelsey, p. 143).

In mental illness.—The fact that nonreligious tongues speaking often occurs in association with certain mental illnesses is well documented. Psychiatrists have reported it in association with schizophrenia, neurosis, and psychosis. Probably all psychiatrists and psychologists are aware of the possibility of psychic damage resulting from tongues speaking (Kelsey, p. 227). It was reported that following the extended tongues meetings held by Aimee Semple McPherson, founder of the Church of the Foursquare Gospel, mental institutions in the area of her meetings were overburdened. The Episcopalian church financed a study commission which concluded that tongues are "not *per se* a religious phenomenon" and may appear among those "who are suffering from mental disorders as schizophrenia and hysteria" (Jennings, p. 11).

In spiritism.—Tongues speaking occurs among anti-Christian spiritistic mediums. Contrary to *popular* belief among tongues speakers, a few years ago the European Pentecostal Conference admitted that "tongues might occur apart from the Spirit's action" (Brown, p. 151).

In the demon possessed.—Even Pentecostal authors grant that there are cases where demonic influence is apparently responsible for tongues utterances. Some feel that this is why "the gift of discernment of spirits" is necessary.

In doctrinal deviates.—Tongues speaking occurs among liberals and others who deny the inspiration of the Scriptures, the Virgin Birth, the substitutionary atonement, the doctrine of creation, and other vital doctrines. One young man who spoke in tongues at Yale University later admitted that he was not a believer at all at the time (Hitt, p. 3). Marcus Bach, a leading advocate of tongues, denies the personality of the Holy Spirit and teaches that "all roads that lead to God are good" (pp. 115, 182). The United Pentecostal Church is so named because it denies the doctrine of the Trinity. Roman Catholics who teach that salvation comes through the sacraments, thereby denying that it comes through faith alone, are receiving this experience. Tongues are often associated with visions and prophecies that are contradictory to the revealed Word of God.

Blasphemous utterances.—Dr. A. C. Gaebelein reported a tongues speech which included words in a Chinese dialect which were too "vile and obscene" to be repeated, according to a missionary who was present (Bauman, p. 42). A speaker on another occasion was described as "blaspheming the Lord Jesus Christ in a most awful manner" (McCrossan, p. 33). Similar reports have been given by others. V. Raymond Edman, a former president of Wheaton College, reported that during their ritual dances Tibetan monks have spoken in English, including profanity typical of drunken sailors (Jennings, p. 13). Many have felt that such instances prove demonic influence. This possibility cannot be ignored, but another explanation will be offered in a later chapter.

Immorality.—This is a distasteful subject to bring up—

especially since so many people who speak in tongues are sincere Christians seeking a closer relationship with God and attempting to live unreproachably. Nevertheless, immorality *has* often followed closely on the trail of tongues utterances. This was the case even among the Corinthians—a most carnal church. The Cevenols were charged with promiscuity, as were tongues speakers at Loudon, the French Prophets in London, and a few of the Irvingites.

The doctrines of free love and "spiritual marriages" have too often appeared in association with tongues. Perversion of the Biblical teaching relating to sex and marriage can be seen in the Mormons and the Shakers. Aimee Semple McPherson was not the only tongues leader to receive a "revelation" that her marriage was "not in the Lord" and that she should enter another union. One of the serious problems of the Pentecostal movement has been the fact that many of its leaders have fallen into immorality. One well-known Pentecostal preacher, a woman widowed for three years, professed to be "with child of the Holy Ghost." Parham, "father of the modern Pentecostal movement," was arrested for the grossest of immoralities (Bauman, p. 34). Bauman quotes one young man as saying, "To my surprise, I found that these blessed emotions in my soul seemed to be accompanied with sexual passion in my body" (p. 37).

By no means should these facts cause one to conclude that all who speak in tongues are involved in sexual immorality. They do show that the two experiences, tongues and illicit passions, are not incompatible. The human mind (or heart) is desperately wicked, and to forego conscious self-control is to invite the subconscious passions to run rampant. Frequently immoral relationships have been "justified" by explaining that the love being manifested is "not of the flesh, but of the Spirit"; besides "in Christ Jesus there is neither male nor female." It is noteworthy that tongues occurred among the worshipers of "Father Divine," who was noted both for his acceptance of worship as God and for his sexual promiscuity with his devotees.

Summary

Tongues occurred before Pentecost, and they have occurred since among both Christian and non-Christian groups. Except for the heretical Montanists, there is no clear evidence of any Christian groups practicing tongues between A.D. 55 and the seventeenth century. But during this time, and continuing to the present day, tongues have frequently been a part of non-Christian religious practices. Beginning in the seventeenth century, tongues groups appeared again in Christian circles. Most of them, however, were eventually discredited by orthodox Christianity for improper behavior, doctrinal deviation, or both. The Pentecostal movement began in 1901, tongues entered the mainline denominations in 1960, and this experience is now being practiced and sought by many throughout the world.

Tongues are not a self-authenticating phenomenon. The fact that one speaks in tongues, in itself, proves nothing. This will lend weight to later considerations suggesting that tongues are a psychological phenomenon possible for any human being by virtue of the fact that he is human. Whether Christian or non-Christian, spiritual or unspiritual, *anyone* can speak in tongues.

CHAPTER 2

The Nature of Tongues

Throughout the Church Age Biblical scholars have held contrasting opinions as to the nature of the tongues utterances described in the New Testament. Many, emphasizing that at least in Acts 2 foreign language elements were clearly involved, have concluded that the gift of tongues was always a miraculous speech in a foreign language. Others, impressed by the statements in 1 Corinthians 14 that no one ever understood a tongues utterance (v. 2) and that the mind was not being exercised (vv. 14-19), have concluded that tongues were always a kind of unintelligible gibberish Unfortunately, some proponents of this view consequently decided that Luke's explanation of the events of Pentecost was inaccurate. Still other scholars have asserted that the 1 Corinthians tongues were not foreign languages and were unintelligible, whereas the Acts 2 tongues consisted of clear discourses in foreign languages. One thing is clear: when spiritually-minded and capable scholars hold such diverse opinions, only prejudice and false pride can lead to hasty conclusions.

This chapter will present evidences that the New Testament indicates that tongues always consisted of unintel-ligible utterances, not "languages" in the normal sense of that word, but that words and phrases of foreign lan-guages *could* occur in any such utterance. The mechanics or methods by which this is accomplished will be dis-cussed in later sections.

Did God Err?

The most common view among evangelicals, and that which was formerly held by this writer, is that in the genuine gift of tongues God miraculously caused a person to speak in a real language he had not learned in order to convey a message to speakers of that language. This means that the genuine gift involved a definite miracle.

Yet it is clear that in writing to the Corinthians Paul was seeking to correct the *misuse* of a legitimate spiritual gift. He did not suggest that some had a real gift whereas others had a substitute or were imitating. He granted that the speaker was praying with his spirit, giving thanks well, and edifying himself (1 Cor. 14:2, 14-17); he was just not edifying others. Paul's point was that the Corinthians were misusing the gift—speaking in tongues at the wrong time and wrong place. Practically every author admits this.

The contradiction should be apparent. If speaking in tongues involved a supernatural speech in a real language, then every such utterance required a direct miracle by God. This would mean, in the case of the Corinthians, that God was working a miracle at the wrong time and wrong place! *He* was causing that which He was directing the Apostle Paul to curtail!

It will not do to say that the gift of tongues was a *permanent* endowment of ability to speak in an un-learned foreign language. There is no Biblical precedent for anyone being given a "store" of miraculous divine power. In fact, this is inconceivable. A divine miracle, by definition, requires a direct and immediate exertion of divine energy. Paul was apparently endowed with all the spiritual gifts, certainly the gift of tongues (1 Cor. 14:19), yet he did not have permanent power to work miracles. They were all done when and as *God* did them. Though Paul had the gift of tongues, he preached to the Gentiles in the common Greek, not in their native languages or dialects. When the people at Lystra, impressed by a miracle, began to worship Paul, it is clear that he did not understand the "speech of Lycaonia," and apparently his own speech had been misunderstood (Acts 14:6-18).

The tongues at Corinth, though they were really tongues, were not miraculous, because God cannot err by working a miracle at the wrong time and place.

The Uniqueness of Pentecost

No Christian should ever lose sight of the uniqueness of Pentecost. Just ten days earlier Jesus had told the apostles that they would receive power when the Holy Spirit would "come upon them" (Acts 1:8). Accordingly, as the apostles waited they anticipated something unusual. When the Day of Pentecost arrived, the twelve apostles (not the 120 disciples who had met earlier to elect Matthias as a replacement for Judas) were in the upper room. Suddenly they heard the sound of a rushing, mighty wind, and tongues of fire descended and sat upon each of the twelve. Then the Holy Spirit caused them to speak in tongues. This unusual sound quickly attracted a crowd, the various members of which were able to recognize ascriptions of praise to God in their native languages.

Pentecost can no more be repeated than can the crucifixion and resurrection of Christ. This unique occasion is properly called the birthday of the Church. On this day baptism with the Spirit was begun. Spirit baptism is the divine ministry which places one in the Body of Christ, the Church. The wind and fire were unique to that occasion. Likewise, it is *possible* to consider the tongues on that occasion as uniquely miraculous or as at least *containing* a miraculous element not later repeated. Due to the singularity of Pentecost this possibility should never be denied. On the other hand, no one would say that Peter's speech which followed was "miraculous," though the Holy Spirit caused it and guided Peter's thoughts. Perhaps the same statements can be made regarding the tongues utterances. This possibility will be explained in succeeding sections.

Lexical Authorities

Because the Greek word *glōssa* ("tongue") sometimes means "language," some have argued that in tongues passages this must be its meaning. It is striking, however, that *every* Greek lexicon, or dictionary, states that the word is also used for unintelligible ecstatic utterances. All of the standard lexical authorities have so understood tongues. It just is not true that when the word does not refer to the physical organ it must refer to a language spoken by some group of individuals.

The Common Conception

There can be no question that in Greek literature during the Apostolic Age, the concept of "speaking in tongues" was understood as "speaking unintelligibly," not as speaking in a foreign language. One example is a story about Job's daughters. The apocryphal *Testament of Job*, written by a Jewish author, probably dates from shortly after the Maccabean period. There were revisions, probably by a Jewish Christian, sometime during the first two centuries of the Christian Era. This fictitious work records that Job gave each of his three daughters a magic girdle. The first put hers on and "immediately became outside her own flesh . . . and received another heart so as no longer to think the things of the earth, she spoke out . . . in the tongue of the angels" (See Kittel, I, 723, and Orr, I, 177). (The words "spoke out" are a translation of the same word rendered "utterance" in Acts 2:4.) The second daughter spoke in the "language [*dialektos,* as in Acts 2:6] of principalities," and the third spoke in the "language of cherubim." All three, in these differing angelic languages, were singing (same word as in 1 Cor. 14:15) and blessing God and telling of "the wonderful works of God" (same phrase in Acts 2:11).

Because they were unintelligible, tongues were often conceived of as a heavenly or angelic language. Some people today think the same thing about their own tongues. Apparently some of the Corinthians, also, knowing that their tongues were unintelligible, believed that they were speaking in an angelic language. Paul responded, "Even though I *should* speak [which I do not] in [all] the languages of men and of angels," without love it would not be profitable.

Tongues in Mark 16:17

As one of the signs associated with the apostolic ministry, our Lord predicted, "They shall speak with new tongues." The word "new" here *(kainos)* stresses the concept of *difference*, or newness in *quality* (Abbott-Smith, p. 226). This would certainly be more appropriate for describing unintelligible ecstatic utterances than existing foreign languages. An even more significant problem for the foreign language view is the questionable textual status of this word. It is omitted in Codex Ephraemi Rescriptus and a number of other important manuscripts. The important manuscripts Vaticanus and Sinaiticus are not witnesses against this omission since they omit the whole passage. The great textual scholars Westcott and Hort relegated this word to their footnotes.

Consequently, it is possible that Jesus only said, "They shall speak in tongues." If this is the case, tongues *must* be understood as ecstatic utterances. The statement, "They shall speak in languages," would be nonsense, since people always speak in languages.

Tongues in 1 Corinthians

There are numerous evidences in 1 Corinthians 12—14 that the tongues mentioned were not real languages. It is not possible in a work of this size to present all of them. Only a few of the major evidences will here be outlined.

1 Corinthians 13:8.—This verse simply states that "Tongues . . . shall cease." The language view asserts that the word "tongues" *(glōssa)*, when not referring to the physical organ, always means "languages" (Bellshaw, p. 147). But the statement, "Languages shall cease," would be difficult to understand and apparently untrue. The statement, "Unintelligible ecstatic utterances shall cease," would make good sense.

Of course the passage is speaking of spiritual gifts, and the statement, "The gift of speaking in unlearned languages shall cease," would be just as understandable as the statement, "The gift of speaking in unintelligible ecstatic utterances shall cease." The point is simply that it cannot be said that the Greek word *glōssa* must in references to tongues always be translated "languages."

1 Corinthians 14:2.—According to Paul, no one could understand a person speaking in tongues. This is an absolute statement, with no qualification. Those holding the language view must insert a qualifying phrase such as, "No man *present at the service* understands him"

(Gromacki, p. 63).

The word "unknown."–The word "unknown" in chapter 14 is an insertion by the King James translators. Believing that tongues were always foreign languages, they were compelled to insert this word to indicate an "unknown" foreign language–that is, one which the speaker had not learned. In fact, anyone who holds the language view *must* make such a textual or at least conceptual emendation to the text. The words of the New Testament, as they stand, will not allow the language view. For example, in 14:2 Paul states that "he that speaketh in a tongue speaketh not unto men." If "tongue" meant a foreign language, the statement would read, "He that speaketh in a *language* speaketh not unto men." This would be difficult to understand, since the primary purpose of language is for communication among men. The language view cannot stand unless a qualifying adjective is inserted in the text.

On the other hand, all of Paul's statements harmonize perfectly with the view being presented. If to speak in a tongue means to speak in an unintelligible ecstatic utterance, the statement would read, "He that speaketh in an unintelligible ecstatic utterance speaketh not unto men." This makes perfectly good sense.

The Interpreter.–If the language view is true, God made another mistake in addition to the mistake of working a miracle at the wrong time. If tongues involved miraculous speech in a foreign language, their purpose was to convey a message; otherwise, the miracle was pointless. But why would God cause someone to speak in a language not understood by anyone present? Did He make a mistake? Did He therefore have to work *another* miracle to give a miraculous translation to some "interpreter"? How could a foreigner be impressed by such?

Why didn't God just cause the speech to be in the foreigner's language?

The Corinthian tongues, though not edifying, were never challenged as not genuine even when not interpreted; therefore, their purpose was not to convey a message. Also, if the gift of interpretation involved a miraculous translation, why was it not granted on other occasions, as when Paul and Barnabas did not understand "the speech of Lycaonia" (Acts 14:11)?

The interpreter was not a translator. No one, not even the interpreter, "understood" the utterances (1 Cor. 14:2). (This does not deny that words or phrases could be recognized, but the speech was essentially unintelligible.) Paul's terms *can* sometimes be used of the act of translation, because a translation is an explanation. The specific word for translating, however, is never used with reference to tongues. This word occurs eight times in the New Testament, always with the meaning "translated." Mark 15:34 is an example: *"Eloi, Eloi, lama sabachthani?* which is, being *translated,* My God, my God, why hast thou forsaken me?"* Paul strictly avoided this word, because the interpreter did not translate, rather he gave his impression of the nature and significance of the emotions expressed by the tongues speaker (Alford, p. 580; Godet, II, 266; Kittel, II, 665).

Tongues speaking *never* edified anyone but the speaker (14:4). Even if his utterance was interpreted by another, it was the interpreter who edified, not the tongues speaker. The only way a tongues speaker could edify was to interpret his own utterance. Then it was the interpretation, not the tongues speech, that edified (14:12-13).

Private tongues speaking.—It is *possible* that Paul spoke in tongues in private (14:18-19), and he positively instructed tongues speakers to speak privately, to themselves and to God only, when no interpreter was present (14:28). Again, if tongues were a miraculous speech in a foreign language, why speak to oneself? And what would be the purpose of such a miraculous speech to God? Could not God understand gibberish, or just thoughts, as well as a foreign language? If tongues were foreign languages, it would be reasonable to assume that they were for the purpose of conveying a message to those who understood the language miraculously spoken.

Nonuse of the mind.—In 1 Corinthians 14:14-19 Paul describes tongues speaking as an exercise in which one's "spirit" (probably best understood here as "emotions") is involved, but in which the mind is "unfruitful." He contrasts speaking with the mind (that is, intelligibly, as the result of conscious thought) with speaking unintelligibly and thereby exercising one's "spirit" only. Those who hold the language view generally state that the speaker was thinking in one language but God miraculously caused the utterance to come out in another. To the contrary, this passage indicates that the speaker's mind was not being exercised.

The gifts of prophecy and tongues were in many ways similar. The major difference was that prophecy involved the use of the mind, whereas tongues did not. The prophet spoke rationally in words which both he and his hearers understood; the tongues speaker's utterance was not understood by either the speaker or his hearers. This is why, in the list of gifts in 1 Corinthians 12:8-10, the gift of tongues is classified as a *different kind* of gift from the gift of prophecy. It differed in that the mind was not being employed. Careful students should note that this passage lists gifts rather than various kinds of persons. It is suggested that the use of the dative or instrumental case in the Greek should be translated "*by* one . . . *by* another similar . . . *by* another of a different kind," rather than "*to* one," and so on.

Tongues in Acts 2

As stated earlier, due to the exceptional circumstances of the Day of Pentecost it is conceivable that the tongues on that occasion involved a miracle not included in any other appearance of the phenomenon. No Christian should deny that foreign language elements were at least included in the tongues on that occasion, but there are indications in the text itself that this may not have been *all* that was involved in those tongues utterances. Most of the scholars who wrote on this subject during the first third of the twentieth century held the view herein suggested. It is the writer's conviction that with the more widespread growth of Pentecostalism, the language view became popular among evangelicals who opposed tongues because it so clearly rules out modern tongues. The following considerations will lead to the conclusion that though the Holy Spirit caused the disciples to speak in tongues, their utterances were not necessarily "miraculous," and though any tongues speech might contain words and phrases of foreign languages, the bulk of all such utterances was unintelligible. (The possibility of foreign words and phrases appearing in any tongues utterance will be discussed later.)

The charge of drunkenness.—The author has visited foreign countries and has lived and worked among those who speak another language, but has never known anyone to be accused of drunkenness simply because he spoke in a foreign language. People recognize the existence of other languages and do not consider drunkenness as the explanation for foreign language speech. Especially where the language is recognizable to the hearer would such a thought be alien. If one should hear a straightforward lecture in his own language, the opposite of drunkenness would be presumed. If it was known that the speaker did not know the language he was speaking, this would make the charge of drunkenness even more incredible. Such an event would call for an explanation involving the miraculous—requiring either Satanic or divine power. Neither was suggested by the hearers at Pentecost. They suggested drunkenness (v. 13).

The charge of drunkenness would seem to indicate that there was something very unusual about the speech of the apostles. Peter, who did not hesitate to rebuke his hearers in scathing terms when they were clearly blamable (v. 23), did not rebuke them at all for this charge. He merely responded, "These are not drunken, as ye suppose, seeing it is but the third hour of the day" (v. 15).

The verb "laleō."—Acts 2:4 states that the apostles "began to *speak* with . . . tongues." The verb "speak" *(laleō)* used here and in every other reference to tongues speaking is very significant. Lexical authorities are unanimous in pointing out a distinction between the synonyms *laleō* and *legō*. *Laleō* refers simply to the fact of utterance, whereas *legō* refers to rational or logical expression (Kittel, Trench, Arndt and Gingrich, Moulton and Milligan, *et al.*). In classical Greek *laleō* commonly means to "prattle" or "babble," and in compounds this is always its meaning—the opposite of normal or rational speech (Kittel, IV, 3, 76). The Scriptural phrase, "He spake . . . saying" (Mt. 13:3; Lk. 24:6-7 and others) illustrates the usage of these words. The first word, "spake" *(laleō)*, simply indicates that He opened His mouth and made utterance. The second word, "saying" *(legō)*, points to the content of what was said. Trench was convinced that there is no "passage in the New Testament where the distinction between them has not been observed" (p. 288).

The use of these terms in Acts 2 is instructive. In every case where the utterances of the tongues speakers are described, forms of *laleō* are used (vv. 4, 6, 7, 11). In every case where the words of the hearers are described, forms of *legō* are used (vv. 7, 12, 13). These words were chosen by the Holy Spirit, and the change in terminology was purposeful. The interchanging of words, with the fact that *legō* is never used for tongues speaking, certainly favors the view that tongues were ecstatic utterances, mostly unintelligible, and not rational expressions.

Strange tongues.—In the Authorized Version, Acts 2:4 says that the apostles began to speak with "other" tongues. The word "other" is *heteros*. It means "another of a different kind." Trench insisted that the difference it designates is always a difference for the worse (p. 360). It is better to say that it *generally* indicates inferiority but *always* indicates a marked difference. The synonym *allos* means "another of the same or similar kind."

Probably the most familiar passage contrasting these two terms is Galatians 1:6-7. There Paul expressed his wonder that the Galatians were so quickly moving from the true gospel to a "different" *(heteros)* gospel, which was not "another" *(allos)* gospel, for there is no "other" *(allos)* gospel. One may preach a "strange" or a "different" gospel, but he cannot preach "another" gospel!

Similarly, our Lord was led away with two "others," criminals, to be crucified (Lk. 23:32). The word is *heteros.* The use of *allos* here would actually have been blasphemous. When Jesus promised to send the Holy Spirit, He called Him "another" Comforter of the same nature *(allos)*, not a "different" kind (Jn. 14:16). When Jesus walked with the two disciples on the road to Emmaus, He appeared in a strange *(heteros)* form so that they did not recognize Him (Mk. 16:12). Likewise, in Jude 7, Sodom and Gomorrah and the angels that sinned are accused of going away after "strange" *(heteros)* flesh, not just "other" flesh.

The distinction between these terms always holds good, though there is one reference which at first glance appears to contradict this. In 1 Corinthians 14:21 Paul uses *heteros* in a compound word to describe the speech of the Assyrians as referred to by Isaiah. According to Trench (p. 360) and others, however, the term *heteroglōssa* really means "a barbarous tongue," indicating inferiority and contempt. Even here the major emphasis is upon unintelligibility. The normal way to say "another tongue" was by *alloglōssa*, as in the Greek translation of Ezekiel 3:6.

If Luke (a Greek) had meant that the apostles spoke in "other" languages, he would have used *allos*. But under the guidance of the Holy Spirit he chose to say that they spoke in "different" or "strange" *(heteros)* languages. Trench concluded properly that by the choice of this term the Holy Spirit was designating the tongues as "quite different in kind from any other speech of men" (p. 359).

Spirit-caused utterance.—Acts 2:4 states that the apostles began to speak in tongues "as the Spirit gave them utterance" (A.V.). The word translated "utterance" *(apoptheggomai)* is not a noun, but an infinitive. It is a compound word with the basic meaning "to produce a sound" or "to call out loudly." The preposition *(apo)* intensifies this concept, suggesting an impassioned utterance or one with unusual fervor and enthusiasm.

The word occurs two other times in the New Testament. In Acts 2:14 it introduces Peter's Pentecostal sermon; he "lifted up his voice and spoke fervently to them." Paul once spoke with such fervor that Festus accused him of being mad with much learning (Acts 26:25). Paul's defense was, "I am not mad ... but *fervently speak* the words of truth and soberness."

In extrabiblical literature this word was used to describe the "inspired" utterances of diviners. Moulton and Milligan cite three occurrences of the word in Vettius Valens where it designates irrational or unintelligible speech. It is stated that the speakers' minds had "fallen away," they were overcome with "madness," and they spoke in "ecstasy" (p. 72). *Apoptheggomai* was almost a technical term for describing the speech of oracle-givers, diviners, prophets, exorcists, ecstatics, and other "inspired" persons (Kittel, I, 447; Arndt and Gingrich, p. 101). The basic idea is "an unusual utterance by virtue of inspiration." Though the word obviously cannot be limited to unintelligible speech, it is certainly appropriate for such. Its usage in Greek literature, in fact, definitely suggests a connection with ecstatic, often unintelligible, utterances.

The context here in Acts 2, with what is said about tongues in 1 Corinthians, supports this concept. The following translation is thus entirely plausible: "They began to speak in strange tongues as the Spirit gave [caused] them to speak ecstatically."

An unnecessary miracle.—It was not necessary for the Jews dwelling in Jerusalem on the Day of Pentecost to be addressed in their native languages. They understood Peter's speech in Aramaic, and it was his speech that brought three thousand to salvation—not the tongues utterances. The response to the tongues utterances was not belief, but the charge of drunkenness. Ecstatic utterances would have served the same purpose as a miraculous foreign language speech, that is, they were simply a sign to call attention to an unusual "inspirational" experience. Only Peter's explanation, in Aramaic, clarified the matter.

It should also be observed that the tongues speaking began *before* any outsiders arrived. The crowd was apparently attracted by this sound (v. 5). Miraculous speech in a foreign language when no foreigners were present would seem to be unnecessary.

Essential Identity

It has been demonstrated above that in Luke's description of the Pentecostal tongues there are indications that they were not just straightforward lectures in foreign languages. The tongues in Corinth were clearly ecstatic and unintelligible, though there is an indication in 1 Corinthians that they also may have included occasional foreign words or phrases. This is all that need be asserted with regard to the Pentecostal tongues. Apart from compelling evidence to the contrary, it should be assumed that all cases of Biblical tongues were essentially identical. There is no such evidence.

The following considerations lend further support to the conclusion that all Biblical references to tongues should be understood as describing an essentially identical phenomenon.

(1) 1 Corinthians was written about A.D. 55 and Acts about A.D. 63. It would seem strange that Luke would use the same terminology (particularly *glōssa* and *laleō*) for the phenomenon which Paul had already discussed so thoroughly if by it he was describing a different experience.

(2) The close association of Luke and Paul (2 Tim. 4:11) would make the preceding point even more meaningful.

(3) While Paul was at Ephesus he wrote to the Corinthians (1 Cor. 16:8), yet nowhere in his lengthy instructions did he suggest that their tongues were in any

way different from those he witnessed upon his arrival at Ephesus (Acts 19).

(4) Nothing in Luke's account of the Ephesian tongues in Acts 19 suggests that they differed from those he described earlier in his book.

(5) The tongues in Acts 10 were certainly essentially identical to those in Acts 2, for Peter stated that "the Holy Spirit fell on them as on us at the beginning" (11:15) and they received a "like gift" ("equal") to that received by the apostles at Pentecost.

(6) The Gospel of Mark was written after the events of Pentecost were well known, and perhaps after 1 Corinthians and Acts had been circulated for several years. In his translation of Jesus' prediction about tongues in association with the apostolic ministry, Mark employed the same verb and noun used by Paul and Luke. He gave no hint that the tongues predicted by Jesus were any different from either those witnessed at Pentecost or those witnessed later.

Conclusion

All the evidence suggests that Biblical tongues were in all cases ecstatic utterances and essentially unintelligible. Any such utterances (today as well) may occasionally have included foreign words or phrases, but these were only bits and pieces in the mass of unrecognizable sounds. As will be demonstrated later, this phenomenon is psychologically explainable. Only on the unique occasion of Pentecost is there clear warrant for assuming that the Holy Spirit guided in the choice of the recognizable phrases.

CHAPTER 3

The Purpose of Biblical Tongues

The intent of this chapter is to examine the various theories as to the purpose of the gift of tongues as it is described in the New Testament. Six common theories will be evaluated and a seventh will be suggested as the purpose best agreeing with the Biblical record.

First Theory: Church Edification

According to this view, the gift of tongues was and is given for the purpose of edifying other believers. The whole purpose of 1 Corinthians 14:1-19, however, is to emphasize that tongues were worthless for this purpose. Actually, tongues *never* "edified" anyone but the speaker (v. 4). When they were interpreted, the *interpretation* could edify. Only when the tongues speaker *himself* interpreted his utterance was he in any sense equal to the prophet (vv. 5, 12-13). Even then, the equality was only that both edified, not that they edified to the same degree.

Greek scholars have frequently pointed out that the Authorized Version's translation of verse 6 may obscure Paul's meaning. His meaning is, "If I should come to you speaking in tongues, what shall I profit you? The only way I can profit you is by speaking either by revelation, or by knowledge, or by prophecy, or by teaching." Accordingly, Lenski has pointed out that "no revelation, knowledge, prophecy, or teaching were ever couched in the strange idiom of tongues" (p. 583). Apparently the "edification" offered by an interpretation of tongues was only that others could share the emotion being expressed and rejoice in the praise being offered (v. 16).

In verse 19 Paul explicitly stated that when addressing an assembly of believers *(ekklēsia),* he would prefer to speak only five intelligible words with his understanding than innumerable (literally) words in a "tongue." It is clear that tongues were not given for the purpose of edifying, instructing, or enlightening other believers.

Second Theory: Evangelization

The most common view among evangelicals is that tongues were intended as a means to get the gospel to foreigners in their own languages. This is considered to be proved by the events at Pentecost and by Paul's statement that tongues serve as a sign with reference to unbelievers (14:22). The following difficulties argue against this view.

Lack of evidence

The New Testament offers no evidence that tongues ever served to evangelize anyone. This was not their purpose at Pentecost, for the converts were not won by the tongues but by Peter's sermon. The tongues began before the crowd arrived. If their purpose was evangelism, the apostles would have been preaching the gospel to one another in an effort to evangelize one another (see Scroggie, pp. 34-35). This hardly seems likely and certainly is not necessary.

The tongues at Caesarea were certainly not for evangelization, for it was the new Christians who spoke in
tongues, and no unsaved persons were present (Acts
10:44). At Ephesus, also, there is no intimation that any
unsaved persons were present. And the Corinthian
tongues were clearly not evangelistic. In fact, Paul remarked that unbelievers observing them would likely be
repelled, just as they were at Pentecost (1 Cor. 14:23;
Acts 2:13).

No indication of gospel content

Tongues speeches are never described as containing any
reference to the gospel. The Acts 2 listeners did not hear
of the substitutionary death, the burial, and the resurrection of Christ, but of "the wonderful works of God."
The term translated "wonderful works" *(megaleia)* is a
familiar term in the Septuagint for Jehovah's mighty
deeds on behalf of His people (e.g., Deut. 11:2; Ps.
71:19). In Acts 10 a word from the same root is employed. It is stated that "they heard them speak with
tongues, and magnify God." It is not clear whether the
phrase "magnify God" refers to the tongues speeches or
to *additional* utterances. Perhaps Peter and his friends
just understood that in their tongues the Gentiles were
magnifying God. There is no indication of any foreign
language elements as in Acts 2.

Paul referred to tongues as though they consisted of
praying and singing with one's spirit. He did not intimate
that they ever contained the gospel or were useful for
evangelism.

Paul's argument

The argument of 1 Corinthians 14:20-25 is that

tongues were not intended to evangelize the unsaved and could, in fact, be positively harmful to this purpose. Three lines of evidence can be cited in support of this conclusion.

A malicious use.—In verse 20 Paul suggests that the Corinthians were being immature in their emphasis upon tongues and urges them in their thinking on this subject to be mature, but in *malice* to be as babies. The implication is obvious. Their use of tongues was having malicious results. True, it was not "malice aforethought," but their tongues were repelling and thus damning unbelievers rather than attracting them to the gospel.

A historical illustration.—Paul's "star witness" in verse 21 is Isaiah. When the Jewish people refused to heed Isaiah's plain words to them he responded that God would consequently "speak" to them by causing them to hear the strange (and, to them, unintelligible) tongue of the Assyrians. Because they refused to heed plain speech they would hear unintelligible speech; they would be subjugated by the Assyrians.

Meyer (p. 20) and Alford (II, 596) both remarked that the two occurrences of the adjective "unbelievers" and the two occurrences of the participle "believing ones" are all datives of reference. To address people in an unintelligible language was not necessarily to give *to them* a sign, but it was a sign *with reference to them,* marking them out as unbelievers who would not accept a plain message. Paul certainly did not consider tongues to be of value as a sign *to* unbelievers, for he states in verse 23 that unbelievers would conclude that the tongues speakers were mad. Also, the present tense participles, "believing ones," designate those who are believing at the time of hearing. The participles are in contrast to the adjectives, "unbelievers," which designate those already in a settled state of unbelief. Consequently, Paul's conclusion based on the illustration from Isaiah is that "tongues serve as a sign, not with reference to those who are believing [what they hear] but with reference to those who are unbelievers." It should be obvious that one cannot be led to belief by speech which he cannot understand!

The statement that tongues are for a sign with reference to "them that believe not" does not mean that they served to *convert* unbelievers, rather the opposite is indicated. In Isaiah's prophecy unintelligible language was for those who had rejected clear speech; "yet for all that will they not hear me, saith the Lord" (v. 21). The *only* purpose of the illustration is to say that in the case of the Corinthian tongues, just as in Isaiah's case, unintelligible speech was not for those who were believing, but for unbelievers who would still not be brought to belief by the unintelligible speech. This illustration was not intended to teach any other point about the nature or purpose of tongues—only that people will not be converted by tongues utterances.

A practical illustration.—Verse 23 depicts an ideal situation as far as the Corinthians were concerned, that is, *all* being gifted with tongues and *all* using this gift in their assemblies. Alford, Lenski, Kling, and other Greek scholars have remarked that this does not suggest a tumultuous or simultaneous babel, but the *best* use of tongues as conceived by the Corinthians—*all* gifted, and speaking in due order one after the other. Paul stated that even with such an overwhelming (from the Corinthian viewpoint) display of tongues, unbelievers would be repelled and driven away. Even the "untaught ones," the interested unbelievers or catechumins, would be repelled.

Third Theory: Condemnation

A few scholars have contended that tongues were intended to serve as a sign of judgment or condemnation upon unbelievers because of their unbelief. This view is based upon a misinterpretation of 1 Corinthians 14:21-22. These verses have been properly evaluated above.

Obviously, to address an unbeliever *only* in tongues would in a sense be a judgment upon him, for he could not be saved in this manner. But this was not the purpose of tongues. Tongues definitely did not serve to condemn unbelievers at the house of Cornelius, or at Ephesus. No unbelievers were present.

Fourth Theory: A Sign to Israel

A common contention among evangelicals opposed to tongues is that they had a unique purpose for Israel only. Consequently, modern tongues, since they are not addressed to Israelites, are unbiblical. (This is often held along with the theory that tongues were for evangelization.) This theory is based solely on 1 Corinthians 14:21-22, which states that the strange tongues of Isaiah's prophecy were addressed to "this people." Since the next verse states that "tongues are for a sign . . . to them that believe not," some people conclude that tongues were for unbelieving Jews only.

This view runs into immediate conflict with the accounts in Acts 8, 10 and 19. When those tongues occurred, no unbelievers of any nationality were present. The usual harmonization attempted is to assert that "them that believe not" was not limited to unsaved Jews, but included also saved Jews with weak faith or some kind of doubt about the gospel or God's program for this age. In evaluating this concept three further matters should be given consideration:

A major difficulty with this view is that the adjective which should be translated "unbelievers" in 1 Corinthians

14:22 cannot possibly mean believers who have weak faith. The same unbelievers are described in verses 24 and 25 (same word) as those who may be led to salvation.

Also, though Isaiah was addressing Jewish people, the words "this people" do not designate Jewish people as such, but *unbelieving* Jewish people. Paul's conclusion is *not*, "Wherefore tongues are for a sign to the Jews," but, "Wherefore tongues are for a sign . . . with reference to the unbelievers."

The strange speech mentioned by Isaiah was spoken to Jews by the pagan Assyrians. The same logic which takes this illustration from Isaiah as requiring that tongues be addressed to Jews only should for the same reason require that tongues be spoken only by pagan Gentiles! This was certainly not the case at Pentecost or at Ephesus, where apparently only Jews were present.

There is a third problem with this view. The Corinthian believers were mostly Gentiles. Paul opened his discussion about the Corinthian tongues by saying, "Ye know that ye were Gentiles . . ." (12:2). In all his discussion about the gift, including his list of restrictions (14:27-34), he never suggested that they should speak in tongues only when Jews were present.

Fifth Theory: Proof of Spirit Baptism

Proponents of tongues speaking nearly always view it as proof of "the baptism with the Holy Ghost," as it is commonly called. Most speak of tongues as the *only* Scriptural proof of "the baptism." Those who hold this position consider "infilling," "filling," "that mighty enduement," and "receiving the Holy Ghost" to be synonyms for the baptism with the Holy Spirit. Some, however, understand the term "baptism" as referring only to the *first* filling.

The word "filling" in Pentecostalism always presup-

poses a baptism, whether the "baptism" happens once
with the first filling or recurs with every filling. Yet in the
New Testament many believers are said to be filled with
the Holy Spirit, or to have received the Holy Spirit, without the slightest indication that they spoke in tongues.

"Baptized" without tongues

Peter promised that those who accepted his Pentecostal message would "receive the gift of the Holy Spirit"
(Acts 2:38), so it is proper to assume that they did, but
there is no hint that any of the 3,000 converts spoke in
tongues. Acts 4:31 states that "the place in which they
were assembled was shaken, and they were all filled with
the Holy Spirit." As a result, "they were speaking the
Word of God with boldness." Not one word is said about
tongues. So one might proceed through Acts and through
the New Testament. It is just not true that tongues are
presented as an essential proof of the reception, baptism,
filling, or "infilling" of the Spirit. The explicit terms
"filled with" or "full of" the Spirit are used nine times in
Acts, and only in Acts 2 is there any connection of these
terms with tongues.

Confusion of terms

In tongues circles "getting the baptism" is commonly a
euphemism or honorific term for "speaking in tongues."
Theologically, in their view, the baptism is not the
tongues speaking, but tongues are the only infallible attestation to the baptism. Four matters need to be understood.

Spiritual baptism.—It is true that the tongues at Pentecost and at Caesarea, though they were not the *result* of
Spirit baptism, were in a sense a *proof* of it. Since baptism is a unique work of the Spirit in this age, as its

predictions prove, the tongues (along with the fire and wind at Pentecost) signaled that the Holy Spirit had arrived as promised to *begin* this ministry. The tongues at Caesarea simply proved to Peter and his Jewish friends that the ministry begun at Pentecost was also applicable to Gentiles. Peter's words indicate that tongues had not been appearing regularly among the Jewish believers since Pentecost. He did *not* say, "The Holy Spirit fell on them as He *does* on us," but, "The Holy Spirit fell on them as also upon us *at the beginning.*"

It is instructive to examine the eleven (at most) references to spiritual baptism in the New Testament. Five of these are simply predictions by John and by Jesus that it would take place in the future (Mt. 3:11; Mk. 1:8; Lk. 3:16; Jn. 1:33; Acts 1:5). One is only a statement that it had happened (Acts 11:16). None of these references describes its nature in any way.

To determine its nature, it is necessary to examine the statements about spiritual baptism in the Epistles. There are five such statements and *in each case* the emphasis is on the believer's union with Christ, and the baptism mentioned is a reality for *all* believers, apart from which they are not Christians at all. Commentators on Romans 6:3, regardless of their variation of interpretation, have commonly recognized that this verse refers to a universal baptism of all believers. The phrase "baptized into Christ Jesus" indicates that if one is "in Christ" (the position of all believers of this age; see Ephesians), he is there because of this baptism. It is not a special ministry to a select group of believers.

Galatians 3:26-27 could not be more specific: "For you are all sons of God through faith in Christ Jesus, for as many as were *baptized into Christ* put on Christ."

The statement in Ephesians 4:5, "one Lord, one faith, one baptism," requires not only a single spiritual baptism but also a *universal* baptism of all believers. All in this age who have the one Lord, the one faith, and the one heavenly Father (v. 6) have this baptism.

In Colossians 2:12 believers are said to be "buried together *with Him by the baptism,* with whom also you were raised together through your faith in the operation of God raising Him from the dead." Here baptism unites the believer with Christ and is declared to be accomplished by "faith in the operation of God raising Him from the dead." This is the faith through which salvation comes, and at the moment of such faith the believer is placed in the body of Christ by baptism and is thus united with Christ.

The only other reference to spiritual baptism in the New Testament is in 1 Corinthians 12:13. Here Paul brought up the subject of spiritual baptism to prove to the Corinthians that their emphasis on tongues was wrong. He stated that "by one Spirit we were *all* baptized into one body." He did not mean "all who speak in tongues," for he was addressing all the Corinthians, and he recognized that they did not, and should not, all speak in tongues (12:30). He clearly meant "all believers," as is proved by the following verse.

The reference to spiritual baptism is followed immediately by an illustration about the physical body. A foot cannot be a hand, and an ear cannot be an eye (vv. 14-26). So it is with the body of Christ. The fact that all have been baptized by the Spirit, far from calling for tongues as a proof, proves that not all should speak in tongues. The various members of the body of Christ must function individually, each making his own contribution, not all demonstrating the same abilities. For all to demonstrate the same gifts and abilities would indicate a diseased and uncoordinated body!

Never are tongues said to be the result of Spirit baptism. They are twice said to be a result of the Spirit's "falling upon" persons (Acts 10:44; 11:15). But the falling of the Holy Spirit has no reference to Spirit baptism, for the Holy Spirit "fell upon" men in the Old Testament before His baptizing work began (Ezk. 11:5). Once tongues are said to be a result of being "filled" (Acts 2:4), but they are never associated with the numerous later references to the filling of the Spirit. It must be concluded that the Holy Spirit "fell upon" or "filled" believers and caused them to speak in tongues for a purpose not yet evaluated. Tongues are not the usual or expected concommitant of any of the normal ministries of the Holy Spirit. They do not and did not normally follow either His baptizing or filling ministries.

The baptism is not a filling.—To be filled with the Spirit means that the Holy Spirit has possession and control of the believer. The believer may be assured of this filling if he yields control of himself to the Holy Spirit. Such yieldedness will include self-judgment and confession of sin, submission to the Word, obedience to the guidance of the Spirit, and acceptance in faith of the providential acts of God (Walvoord, pp. 199-202). This ministry of the Spirit is vital for effective Christian worship and service and is available to every believer who will accept it.

The filling of the Spirit is distinct from all His other ministries in the following aspects.

(1) The fact that believers are commanded to be filled with the Spirit (Eph. 5:18) indicates that it is not universal among Christians, whereas all the other ministries, including baptism, are.

(2) The present tense of the command, "keep being filled," indicates that filling should be continuous or repetitive, whereas regeneration, sealing, and baptizing are instantaneous and cannot be repeated.

(3) Only the filling is experiential. The other ministries of the Spirit do not involve time, sequence of experience, or "feelings" (though Christian experiences follow and are based upon them).

(4) Filling is to be especially distinguished from Spirit baptism in that the baptism is a unique ministry begun at Pentecost (Acts 1:5), whereas filling may easily be demonstrated to be a work of the Spirit in the Old Testament, in this age, and in the millennial age.

The confusing label "full gospel" is a misnomer. Anyone who does not have the Holy Spirit is not a Christian (Rom. 8:9, 14; Jude 1-19).

Two spiritual baptisms?—In the Epistles baptism is definitely the universal experience of believers at salvation. Therefore, some have suggested that there are *two* spiritual baptisms: the universal baptism into Christ, which is called the baptism of repentance; and the baptism with the Holy Spirit, or enduement with power, which is signified by tongues (Dake, N.T., p. 2). The first is commonly called the baptism *by* the Holy Spirit, and the second, the baptism *with* or *in* the Holy Spirit.

The first problem with this view is that it is contradicted by Ephesians 4:5, which states that there is only *one* baptism. The second problem is that the distinction between a baptism *by* the Spirit and one *in* the Spirit cannot be sustained. The same Greek preposition *(en)* is used in 1 Corinthians 12:13 as in Acts 1:5.

Part of the confusion on this issue among Pentecostal interpreters is due to their understanding of Jesus' prediction of an enduement with power in Acts 1:8 as an explanation of or as a result of His prediction of the baptism with the Holy Spirit (Acts 1:5). These two are wholly unrelated ministries of the Spirit. Jesus' prediction about the baptism was not even on the same occasion as His prediction about enduement. After the prediction of verse 5, verse 6 states, "So then, *having come together,* they were questioning Him saying, 'Lord, are you at this time restoring the kingdom to Israel?' " His answer follows, and is in turn followed by His prophecy as to the enduement with power. Consequently, the prediction about the baptism and the prediction about enduement are separate prophecies with an unspecified amount of time and a discussion about the kingdom intervening.

"Sign" and "gift."–Tongues advocates generally assert that speaking in tongues "is a most blessed experience that God wishes every Christian to enjoy. It is a normality for all believers" (Horton, p. 26). This is so patently contradicted by 1 Corinthians 12:30, which indicates that not all Christians should speak in tongues, that some attempt at harmonization is essential. Consequently, tongues speakers argue that there are two kinds of tongues, not different in nature but different in cause and purpose.

The Pentecostal position is that the tongues in Acts were a *sign,* but the tongues at Corinth were a *gift.* The *sign* of tongues, they maintain, is the unique seal and proof of the baptism with the Spirit. All Christians, they assert, should seek and expect the *sign,* but not all should expect to receive the *gift.* The *sign* is a proof of the baptism; the *gift* is for continual use in edification. Tongues advocates have called this "the decisive point of the entire controversy," and some have even granted that if this point cannot be sustained, the Pentecostal teaching on tongues cannot be sustained (Brumback, p. 262).

Although some scholars opposing modern tongues have assumed a similar distinction, such a distinction runs counter to the New Testament evidence. In Acts 11:17 a tongues utterance, supposed to be a sign and not a gift, is called a gift. It is the tongues that are designated as the "equal gift" to that at Pentecost, and not the Holy Spirit Himself, because the word "equal" *(isos)* indicates an equality of value or force rather than an equality of identity or quality (Kittel, III, 343). Even more important, Paul did not ask, "Do all have the *gift* of tongues?" His question is, "Do all *speak* with tongues?" His question, in the Greek text, requires "no" as its answer. Not all are supposed to *speak* in tongues in any way. This would include the "sign" as well as the "gift."

The apparent differences between the Corinthian tongues and the Pentecostal tongues may be easily understood without distinguishing between tongues as a sign and tongues as a gift. (Actually, the *gift* of tongues was to serve as a *sign*, as will be demonstrated later.)

The only differences between the tongues in Acts and those at Corinth concern the restrictions placed upon the Corinthian tongues. First, an interpreter was required at Corinth but this requirement is never mentioned in Acts. When it is understood that an interpreter was not a translator, this seeming difference is easily explained. In a sense the tongues at Pentecost were interpreted by Peter. He explained their significance quite adequately (Acts 2:14-36). Peter also interpreted the Caesarean tongues as signifying that Gentiles, as well as Jews, were cleansed and partook fully of the Spirit's ministries and of the gospel as explained by the apostles (10:47; 11:17; 15:8-9). It is reasonable to assume that the significance of tongues at Ephesus and other places was explained ("interpreted") by Paul or by someone else.

Tongues were not intended to convey a message. Paul's restrictions were given *only* because of misuse. If tongues had always been *only* the work of the Spirit, no restrictions would have been needed. Besides, it is possible that in spite of misuse of the gift, God sometimes granted an interpretation—an explanation of the emotions being expressed—in order that the church might gain some benefit. In any case, the restrictions were because of misuse and would apply to any misuse. If the apostles on the Day of Pentecost, had refused to stop speaking in tongues so Peter could deliver his message, or if they had on later occasions attempted to address the church in tongues, it would have been appropriate for some predecessor of Paul to hand them a list of regulations similar to those later given to the Corinthians.

The difference between the tongues at Pentecost and those at Corinth is simply the difference between tongues as caused by the Spirit and used and terminated under His direction, versus tongues as *originally* caused by the Spirit but later misused by carnal Christians.

Conclusion

Tongues are not an essential proof of Spirit baptism; in fact, Spirit baptism regularly occurs without them. The Scriptures never point to tongues as the result of Spirit baptism. Even some Pentecostal writers are aware that their doctrine of tongues as a sign of the "baptism of the Holy Spirit" is not based on a single clear statement in the Word of God. A work published by the Full Gospel Publishing House in Toronto grants that this doctrine is based only upon "circumstantial evidence" deduced from interpretations of the Acts accounts, because "the New Testament contains no plain categorical statement anywhere as to what must be regarded as THE sign" (Gee, pp. 18-19).

Sixth Theory: Devotional

Some people, arguing that Paul spoke in tongues in his private devotional life though not in an assembly of believers gathered for edification (1 Cor. 14:18-19), see tongues speaking as primarily a devotional experience. It is conceivable that one whom the Holy Spirit had caused to speak with tongues could later use this ability in worshiping God. Tongues were definitely devotional in *nature;* however, they were not devotional in *purpose.*

Besides, it is by no means clear that Paul spoke in tongues in private. The common translation of verse 18 is possible, but this verse may also legitimately be translated, "I give thanks to God more than all of you that I speak in tongues." This would require only that Paul had at some time received this gift, could speak in tongues when he desired, and was even more grateful for this gift than were the Corinthians. He did not, however, let his gratitude for the gift cause him to misuse it (v. 19).

Even if Paul did employ tongues in private, this does not mean that believers today should seek tongues as a devotional experience. Paul had originally been given the gift by the Holy Spirit, and, according to our Lord, tongues were caused by the Spirit as a *sign* (Mk. 16:17). As will be demonstrated later, God's Word definitely indicates that since the Apostolic Age the Holy Spirit has not caused anyone to speak in tongues.

Paul's statement in 1 Corinthians 14:18 cannot refer to preaching the gospel in a foreign language or languages (Rice, p. 45). This would require the use of the mind, yet in the next verse he states that he had rather speak only five words with his mind than innumerable words in tongues. His contrast makes it clear that the word "tongues" in both verses refers to the gift of tongues.

There are several indications that tongues were not given as an aid to the believer's devotional experience. In the first place, Paul's lengthy discussion about tongues contains no intimation that tongues provided a *better* means of devotion. On the contrary, he states that he had rather pray and sing with both his spirit *and* his understanding than with his spirit alone—that is, in tongues

(14:14-15).

Again, if the purpose of tongues were devotional, why would the gift *ever* be withdrawn? Throughout eternity saints will be expressing devotion (Rev. 5:13); yet they will not be speaking in tongues (1 Cor. 13:8).

Finally, our Lord's simple statement in Mark 16:17 makes it impossible to believe that tongues were devotional in purpose. He designated tongues as a *sign*. A sign is intended to authenticate or attest to something. On the authority of Jesus Himself it is necessary to conclude that tongues, even if devotional in nature, were not devotional in purpose.

Seventh Theory:
Apostolic Authentication—A Suggested View

Since, on the testimony of Jesus, tongues were a sign, it remains only to determine what they were a sign of. Second Corinthians 12:11-13 gives an important clue. "For I lacked nothing of the chiefest apostles," Paul wrote, "though I am nothing. Indeed, the signs of the apostle were wrought among you in all patience, both by signs, and wonders, and by powerful deeds. For what is there in which you were inferior to the rest of the churches?"

Paul here asserts that following Pentecost every sign, wonder, and powerful deed, that is, every unusual manifestation of the Spirit's presence, was for the purpose of authenticating the apostles as the spokesmen for Jesus—as the revealers of divine truth. He appeals to signs and wonders as the proofs of the apostolic office. If that is what they were, then that is their purpose. And according to God's Word, that is what they were! If such things as casting out demons, miraculous healings, raising the dead, taking up serpents, and speaking in tongues were not the signs of apostleship which Paul had in mind, what *did* he have in mind?

It is important to be aware that after Pentecost no unusual manifestation of the Spirit's presence (no sign) ever occurred except in the presence of an apostle or by those who had been directly ministered to by an apostle. The significance of the apostolic signs will be elaborated in the following chapter.

CHAPTER 4

The Duration
of
Biblical Tongues

How long were Biblical tongues meant to last? This is a legitimate question, and anyone intending to study the subject must face it. Three lines of evidence clearly show what the duration of Biblical tongues was. These are: (1) the major purpose of the gift, which was apostolic authentication, (2) Paul's direct statement that tongues would cease, and (3) the historic fact that tongues did cease.

Apostolic Authentication

The preceding chapter evaluated the various suggestions as to the purpose of the gift of tongues and concluded that the major purpose of tongues, along with the other signs of the Spirit's presence and ministry, was to aid in establishing the authority of the apostles. This being so, their purpose was fulfilled *within* the Apostolic Age. When God had attested the apostles' authority, especially that of the apostle "born out of due time" (1 Cor. 15:8), among representative groups of believers, the signs had served their purpose. They did not even continue through the later years of the apostolic ministry.

This fact can be demonstrated from the following considerations: (1) the distinctive character of the apostolic office, (2) the distinctive purpose of tongues as a sign, (3) the temporary nature of *all* signs, and (4) the temporary nature of *some* gifts.

A distinctive office

The distinctive character of the apostolic office should be emphasized. In the New Testament the apostles are given a place of authority as spokesmen for Jesus which is distinct from that of any other Christians. Five facts clearly show the distinctive character of their office: (1) the fact that the church was founded upon them, (2) the fact that they were eyewitnesses to the resurrection, (3) the fact that they were specially authorized agents, (4) the fact that their appointment was authenticated by signs, and (5) the fact of their apostolic authority.

Foundational.—Ephesians 2:20 states that the church was "built upon the foundation of the apostles and prophets." The word "prophets" does not refer to the Old Testament prophets; rather, the Greek grammar suggests that the church was built upon the apostles *and* New Testament prophets who are here viewed as one group comprising the foundation. It was to these same individuals that the mysteries of the church were revealed (Eph. 3:5). They are clearly said to belong to the foundational stage of the church. The function of the apostles as the major foundational element of the church will be symbolized in the New Jerusalem by the "twelve foundations" which will have "upon them twelve names of the twelve apostles of the Lamb" (Rev. 21:14).

Eyewitnesses.—According to Peter, the primary purpose of an apostle was to serve as "a witness of His resurrection" (Acts 1:22). The Resurrection, of course, proved the validity of all Christ's claims. An apostle had to be one who had seen the risen Lord (1 Cor. 15:7-9). In 1 Corinthians 9:1 Paul asked, "Am I not an apostle?" His immediate justification was, "Have I not seen Jesus our Lord?" Again in 1 Corinthians 15:7-9 this was his vindication of his claim to apostleship: "Afterward He was seen by James, then by all the apostles, and last of all, as to one born out of due time, He was seen by me also. For I am the least of the apostles."

Authorized agents.—Jesus had many disciples. Among His disciples was a select group referred to as "His twelve disciples" (Mt. 10:1), or just "the Twelve" (Mk. 6:7; Lk. 9:1). The fact that they were His followers and pupils did not make them apostles, only disciples. It is significant that the only use of the word "apostle" in Matthew's Gospel is in connection with our Lord's authorization of the Twelve to act as His emissaries: "And having called forward His twelve *disciples,* He gave them *authority*— over unclean spirits, to cast them out, and to heal every disease and every sickness. Now the names of the twelve apostles are these . . ." (Mt. 10:1-2).

The Twelve, "whom also He named apostles" (Lk. 6:13), were so named because of their commissioning as official representatives of Jesus. It was their authorization to act with supernatural power, to act as the representatives of Christ, which merited for them the title, "apostle."

Scholars are not positive whether Jesus spoke with His disciples in Hebrew or in Aramaic. In either language the equivalent of the word "apostle" is a specially significant word. This word (*šaliah* in Hebrew) had a technical legal use. It designated a man commissioned as a representative of another with full legal authority to act on his behalf. He was a proxy. The English words "agent" or "plenipotentiary" in their legal usage have a similar connotation.

The rabbis had a saying, "The šālîaḥ of a man is as the man himself" (Kittel, I, 415).

When Jesus made His twelve disciples "apostles," He told them, "He that receiveth you receiveth me" (Mt. 10:40). They were apostles of Jesus just as Jesus Himself was an apostle of God (Heb. 3:1). An apostle was not just "one sent," but one commissioned to act as an official representative (cf. 1 Kings 14:6, Septuagint).

The word "apostle" is used in the New Testament in two senses, both with the basic concept of a commissioned representative. The primary usage is illustrated by Paul's repeated introduction of himself as "an apostle of the Lord Jesus Christ." This is the highest title conceivable for a mere human (Rev. 21:14). It is not necessary to limit this title strictly to Paul and the Twelve. Barnabas, who was probably one of the seventy and a witness of the resurrected Lord, and James, to whom our Lord paid a special visit after His resurrection, could properly be called apostles (Acts 14:4, 14; 1 Cor. 15:6-7; Gal. 1:19). Even the seventy (or seventy-two) who were sent out and empowered by Jesus might be considered as temporary apostles (Lk. 10:1-20).

The word "apostle" occurs only once in the Gospel of John, only once in Matthew, only once in Mark, and only six times in Luke. It occurs about seventy times in the rest of the New Testament. In view of these facts it might be legitimate to consider the Twelve also as only temporarily authorized as apostles on the occasion mentioned in Matthew 10:1-15. In this case it would be understood that they became permanent, fully authorized apostles on the Day of Pentecost. Paul, of course, later received his appointment to the apostolic office by direct encounter with the risen Christ (Gal. 1:1, 11-12, 16-17; 2:7-8).

In addition to those who were properly "apostles of

the Lord Jesus," at least three men are mentioned as apostles in another sense; they were "apostles of churches" (2 Cor. 8:23, see also Phil. 2:25). This is a "secondary" usage of the term. These apostles were official representatives of specific churches. During the age of the Apostolic Fathers, immediately following the Apostolic Age, Christians dropped this general use of the term and reserved the term "apostle" almost exclusively for those personally chosen by Christ and empowered as His representatives.

Authenticated by signs.—Paul emphasized that his apostleship was not "through man, but through Jesus Christ" (Gal. 1:1). Because "the *šaliah* of a man is as the man himself," the absence of miracles would invalidate the claim of one who asserted that he was an apostle. As part of their commission the apostles were empowered to act on Jesus' behalf. This is why Paul appealed to the "signs of the apostle" (or "signs of apostleship," 2 Cor. 12:12). The signs were "indispensable for the sake of the cause itself, for Jesus' sake" (Kittel, I, 433). The apostles were authenticated for the sake of authenticating their message concerning Christ and His will for the present and future ages.

Because Paul entered the apostolate late, it was especially essential, if his words and writings were to be accepted as authoritative, that all the signs which accompanied the ministry of Peter should also accompany his ministry. He emphasized, in what was probably his first book, that "the one operating [or "energizing"] in Peter unto an apostleship of the circumcision operated also in me unto the Gentiles" (Gal. 2:8).

The great theologian B. B. Warfield pointed out that after Pentecost no unusual manifestations of the Spirit's presence (no *charismata* or signs) ever occurred except on the part of or in the presence of the apostles themselves, or on the part of those upon whom the apostles had laid their hands (pp. 22-23).

Apostolic authority.—The miracles and unusual manifestations of the Spirit's presence which accompanied the apostolic ministry were clearly *signs.* No supposed "healer" since the Apostolic Age has ever healed every one who came to him for healing; yet this occurred in the early part of the apostolic ministry (Acts 5:15-16). Even Peter's shadow was apparently accompanied by healing, as were the handkerchiefs and aprons sent out from Paul through which God accomplished "special miracles" (Acts 19:11-12).

After Ananias and Sapphira died in the presence of Peter, "great fear came upon all the church and upon all those who heard these things. And *through the hands of the apostles* many signs and wonders happened among the people . . . and of the rest, *no one was daring to be joining himself with them, but the people were magnifying them"* (Acts 5:11-13). Because the people were magnifying them, they were "continuing steadfastly in the doctrine of the apostles" (Acts 2:42-43).

The unique authority of the apostles as the revealers of church truth cannot be overemphasized. In his classic work, *The Inspiration and Canonicity of the Bible,* Laird Harris has demonstrated that this was the determinative issue in the canonization of the New Testament books. Only those books which were written by apostles, or by apostolic associates and approved by the apostles, were accepted as authoritative. Warfield stated regarding the Apostolic Fathers (the Church Fathers immediately following the apostles) that "their anxiety with reference to themselves seems to be lest they should be esteemed overmuch and confounded in their pretensions with the Apostles, rather than to press claims to station, dignity, or powers similar to theirs" (p. 10). Ignatius, about A.D.

115, said, "I do not, as Peter and Paul, issue commandments to you. They were apostles. I am but a condemned man" (Roberts, I, 75).

Several tongues groups have been consistent enough to realize that if signs are to be displayed, the office of apostle must be revived. For this reason the Irvingites appointed apostles and named themselves the Catholic *Apostolic* Church.

An apostle could speak with authority. This is why Jude exhorted the early believers to "be mindful of the words which were spoken• by the apostles of our Lord Jesus Christ" (v. 17). This is why Peter placed the *commandments* of an apostle on an equal level with the Old Testament Scriptures (2 Peter 3:2, 15-16). Paul's threat to "come . . . with a rod" is reminiscent of the authority of Jesus in cleansing the temple (1 Cor. 4:21). An apostle could *command* obedience (2 Thess. 3:6, 14). Paul told the Corinthians that a mark of a spiritual man was acknowledgement "that the things that I write unto you are the commandments of the Lord" (1 Cor. 14:37). When Paul said, "we have the mind of Christ," whether the "we" is an editorial "we" or refers to all the apostles, in either case it is an apostolic "we" (1 Cor. 2:16).

Tongues as a sign

Since tongues also occurred in other cultures and religions, one might readily ask how they could serve as a sign to authenticate the apostles.

A part of the answer involves the realization that tongues were consistently thought of as a sign of inspiration. Unless his utterances were understood as merely the babblings resulting from drunkenness, a tongues speaker was thought to be possessed by his god or by some supernatural power.

In addition, it is apparent that any isolated instance of

speaking in tongues on the part of any particular individual would be of very little value as a sign or proof of anything. In all the instances in Acts, where tongues did serve their proper purpose as a sign, the tongues were a spontaneous and simultaneous demonstration by a group (minimum of twelve persons). The fact that in each case the *whole* group *spontaneously* spoke in tongues—when the tongues were interpreted or explained as a demonstration of the Spirit's presence—allowed them to serve as a sign authenticating the truth of the apostolic message.

The following paragraphs will briefly evaluate the significance of tongues as signs in all the passages where they are mentioned in the New Testament.

In Mark 16.—In His post-Resurrection commission to His apostles Jesus predicted tongues as a sign. These signs were to be manifested by the apostles and by those to whom they ministered. Whether the signs were by the apostles or by those who believed what they heard from the apostles, their purpose was to authenticate the apostles as those with the authoritative message and its interpretation. Schaff rightly remarked that "the extension of the statement to believers generally in every age of the church, is not warranted by anything in the text, and introduces confusion. This was a promise to the Apostles and to the apostolic age" (Lange, VIII, 162).

It should be noted that this passage also predicts occurrences of miraculous protection from danger. To seek the experience of tongues because it is predicted as one of the signs in this passage is just as unreasonable as to drink poison or handle snakes because this passage promises protection.

When Mark wrote his gospel, probably about A.D. 68 though the date is now being debated, he considered these signs as past: "But *those* [the apostles], having gone forth, preached everywhere while the Lord worked with them and confirmed the Word through the closely accompanying signs" (v. 20). The only indicative verb form in the sentence is the past tense (aorist) verb "preached." In accordance with Greek syntax, the present tense participles "working," "confirming," and "accompanying" do not represent time subsequent to the apostolic preaching, but time contemporary with it. In fact, Mark was referring only to that apostolic preaching which was accompanied by signs. He knew that this ministry was already past, and he referred to it as such.

In Acts 2.—The church was begun by the non-experiential simultaneous baptism of all living believers into the body of Christ. Though the unusual events at Pentecost signaled this beginning, their primary purpose was to serve as an endorsement of the Twelve. Only the apostles were in the Upper Room, and only they spoke in tongues. The signs especially indicated that the Holy Spirit had arrived to begin those unique ministries with the apostles that Jesus had predicted (Mk. 16:14-18; Jn. 14:26; 16:13). Those dwelling in Jerusalem knew that the speakers were *all Galileans* (Acts 2:7). Peter stood *"with the eleven"* (2:14) when he preached his Pentecostal sermon. After the message, those whose hearts were pricked said to "Peter and to *the rest of the apostles,* Men and brethren, what shall we do?" (2:37). It is then stated that "many wonders and signs were done through the *apostles*" (2:43).

In Acts 8.—Tongues are not explicitly mentioned in this chapter, but it is generally conceded that some such phenomenon occurred on the occasion described here. Philip, who was *not* an apostle but had had the apostles' hands laid upon him (6:6), preached to the Samaritans. Signs and wonders occurred in his personal ministry, but his converts demonstrated no such proofs of divine activity at their own hands. Only when *apostles* came from Jerusalem and laid hands upon Philip's converts was there any unusual demonstration of the Spirit's presence in them.

Peter and John, having gone down, "prayed for them so that they might receive [the] Holy Spirit, for he was not yet fallen upon any of them—only they had been baptized in the name of the Lord Jesus. Then they were laying their hands on them, and they were receiving [the] Holy Spirit" (8:15-17).

This passage, according to Pentecostals, teaches that the Holy Spirit is normally to be received as a special blessing subsequent to conversion. The usual answer to their view is that during this transitional age certain of the normal ministries of the Holy Spirit, such as indwelling, may have been delayed in some cases for special reasons. It is suggested that the Samaritans might have been tempted to begin their own brand of "Christianity" just as they had begun their own brand of "Judaism." To combat this, they were made to recognize the authority of the apostles and obligated to follow apostolic doctrine. This is a legitimate hypothesis.

It is also possible, however, to understand that the Samaritans received all the normal ministries of the Spirit, including Spirit baptism and indwelling, at the moment of their belief, but that there were just no demonstrations or unusual signs of His presence until the laying on of apostolic hands. References to the "falling upon," "coming upon," or "receiving" of the Holy Spirit need not refer to the initiation of His indwelling. They may as easily indicate some unusual manifestation of His presence. Some scholars feel that especially when the article is omitted, as it is in this passage, the emphasis is on the manifestations of His presence. "Falling upon" and "coming upon" are the usual expressions for His filling rather than His indwelling or baptizing ministries.

In any case, whatever manifestation of the Spirit's presence occurred, its purpose was to establish the authority of the apostles among the Samaritans. The signs did not and could not appear apart from the ministry of the apostles. In the following verses Simon was severely rebuked for desiring to purchase this apostolic prerogative. Other passages make it clear that the normal pattern is not for Christians to receive the Spirit at some time subsequent to salvation, for it is stated that if the Holy Spirit does not dwell in a person, that person is not a Christian (Rom. 8:9).

In Acts 10-11.—God employed a series of supernatural visions in order to have Peter be the one to present the gospel to Cornelius and those in his home. The tongues on that occasion were not only an attestation to apostolic authority, but also served to teach Peter something about the exercise of that authority.

In Acts 19.—A problem has arisen here because of the Authorized Version's faulty translation of verse 2: "Have ye received the Holy Ghost since ye believed?" The translation in the American Standard Version is much more accurate: "Did you receive the Holy Spirit when you believed?" The question may even be worded, "Believing, did you receive the Holy Spirit?" This form includes a question about belief as well as about the Spirit. Their answer indicated to Paul that they had not heard all the facts of the gospel, so he told them about the One whom John had predicted. This led to their conversion and baptism in the name of Jesus.

When Paul laid his hands on them, "the Holy Spirit came upon them and they were both speaking in tongues and prophesying" (v. 6). Again, the statement that the Spirit "came upon them" is best understood as referring to an unusual manifestation of His presence rather than to His original arrival. But in this case the manifestation apparently immediately followed His arrival. In any case, the tongues came only after the apostolic ministry and served to authenticate Paul as a properly authorized apostle with a message approved by God.

In 1 Corinthians.—Paul told the Corinthians that the signs of apostleship had been wrought among them *both* by signs *and* by wonders and mighty deeds (2 Cor. 12:12). Apparently, when the Corinthians had been converted under his ministry he had laid his hands upon them and some had been given the gift of tongues. This gift, as well as all the other charismatic gifts, or unusual manifestations of the Spirit's presence, had validated his claim to apostleship and consequently his message. But the Corinthians later misused their God-given ability.

It may be that when Paul wrote to the Romans they had not been ministered to by an apostle and thus had had none of the charismatic gifts displayed among them (like the Samaritans before the apostles came). In writing to them Paul said, "I long to see you, in order that I may impart to you some spiritual gift *[charisma]* that you may be established" (Rom. 1:11).

All signs were temporary

It has been shown that Jesus predicted signs (unusual manifestations of the Spirit's presence or protection) only in association with the apostolic ministry (Mk. 16). Barnes has rightly remarked that "the promise is fulfilled if it can be shown that these signs followed in the case of *any* who believed" (p. 179). Mark considered the signs as past when he wrote in about A.D. 68. Even Peter and Paul, who had previously enjoyed miraculous protection (Acts 12 and 28), had now been executed.

The author of Hebrews in approximately A.D. 68 likewise considered the signs as past: "How shall we escape if we neglect so great a salvation; which at the first began to be spoken by the Lord, and *was confirmed* to us by those who heard Him [i.e., by the apostles]; God also bearing them witness, *both* with signs *and* wonders, and various miracles and distributions of the Holy Spirit according to His will?" (Heb. 2:3-4).

Again, Greek grammar requires that the present tense participle, "bearing witness," represent time contemporary with the past tense (aorist) verb, "was confirmed." The confirmatory signs were clearly considered as already in the past at the time this book was written.

The last miracles recorded in the New Testament took place about A.D. 58 (Acts 28:3-9). Around A.D. 60 Paul's "brother, and companion in labour, and fellow-soldier," Epaphroditus, while visiting Paul became sick "nigh unto death"; but he was not healed miraculously (Phil. 2:25-30). About A.D. 62 Paul's own "true child in the faith" (1 Tim. 1:2) apparently had a stomach ailment which remained uncured (1 Tim. 5:23). Around A.D. 64 one of Paul's associates was so seriously ill that Paul had to leave him behind, uncured (2 Tim. 4:20). Yet earlier, Paul had been instrumental even in restoring life to the dead! Today Christians are not struck dead for lying about their church donations (Acts 5:1-11), and angels do not appear and open prison doors for persecuted Christians (5:19). Even Pentecostals admit that not all the signs, not even all those at Pentecost, are supposed to be regularly repeated.

Some gifts were temporary

All signs may be considered as spiritual gifts, but not all spiritual gifts were signs. (None of the spiritual gifts today are signs.) The gifts of miracles, healings, and tongues were sign gifts. The gifts of apostleship, teaching, evangelism, pastoring, giving, having mercy, and governing were not sign gifts, though apostleship entailed confirmatory signs (1 Cor. 12:28; Rom. 12:3-8; Eph. 4:7-11). All the sign gifts were temporary, and in addition some of the non-sign gifts were temporary. In fact, the most important of such gifts, the gift of apostleship, was temporary.

In 1 Corinthians 12:28 a representative list of gifts is divided into five levels of importance, beginning with apostleship and ending with tongues: "*first* apostles, *second* prophets, *third* teachers, *then* [fourth] miracles, *then* [fifth] gifts of healings, helps, administrations, various kinds of tongues" (NASB). The first three, being explicitly numbered, are of major importance in comparison with the others. It can be proved from Scripture, as Christians generally affirm, that the first two were temporary. If the two most important were temporary, it is certainly possible that the last and least important was also temporary. The fact that it was a sign gift makes this possibility a certainty because the purpose of the signs was to confirm revelation being given.

Paul stated that he was the last one given the gift of apostleship, "the one born out of due time" (1 Cor. 15:8). The church Jesus is building was founded on the apostles. There is no need for apostles today unless the church is to be refounded—and if so, another cornerstone should be required! (See Eph. 2:20).

Tongues Shall Cease

In A.D. 55 Paul pointedly predicted, "Tongues . . . shall cease" (1 Cor. 13:8). The question being debated today is, "When?" For many people the answer hangs on their interpretation of the phrase "that which is perfect" in verse 10. Tongues advocates commonly assume that this is an allusion to the Rapture and conclude that this passage teaches that the gift of tongues and the other gifts mentioned here are to remain in continuance until that great event. Others (including the present writer in previous study) have concluded that this passage specifically, in itself, *proves* that Spirit-caused tongues were limited to the Apostolic Age.

Both of these opinions must be rejected. Paul did not write 1 Corinthians 13:8-13 for the purpose of telling exactly *when* the gift of tongues would cease. His emphasis is merely that tongues and the other gifts he named *would* cease because they were temporary as contrasted with love, in particular, which is permanent. This does not mean that this passage makes no contribution toward answering the question regarding *when* tongues ceased. It means that this question is not answered by this passage *alone.* It has already been demonstrated that the *purpose* of Spirit-caused tongues limits them to the Apostolic Age. The passage under consideration certainly harmonizes with this conclusion and also makes a special contribution in favor of it by intimating that tongues would cease prior to the termination of the two other gifts which are named.

When reference is made to the termination of the gift of tongues it is not meant that the phenomenon never again occurred. Obviously it occurs daily today. What is meant, is that the Holy Spirit stopped causing people to speak in tongues. In the same way, the gifts of apostleship and prophecy were withdrawn, but many people since have claimed apostolic authority and divine origination for their prophetic utterances.

The first step in understanding the predictions of 1 Corinthians 13:8-10 is to identify "that which is perfect."

What is "that which is perfect"?

There are three interpretations which must be evaluated in order to answer this question. The first argues that the Rapture or return of Christ is in view. The second argues that the completion of the New Testament canon is in view. The third argues that the eternal state is in view.

The Rapture.—As stated earlier, those who believe that tongues are a regular ministry of the Spirit throughout the Church Age generally identify "that which is perfect" as a reference to the Rapture. Often, however, the Rapture and the Second Coming are not properly differentiated. Also *some* tongues speakers identify this phrase as a designation for the millennial age which will be ushered in by the coming of Christ (Horton, p. 30). But whether "that which is perfect" is identified as the Rapture, the Second Coming, or the age initiated by these events, these may be considered as really one view for they all understand "that which is perfect" as an event which *follows* the Church Age and *precedes* the millennium. The following considerations will conclusively demonstrate that it is impossible for one who accepts the Bible as authoritative and who examines the Biblical evidence to accept this position.

(1) The term "that which is perfect" cannot refer to the Lord Himself at His coming because the article translated "that which" is neuter, not masculine in gender. Paul really said, "When the perfect *thing* arrives," or "When that *(thing)* which is perfect arrives, that which is partial will be rendered inoperative."

(2) Not only does the neuter gender prohibit the understanding of a personal reference to Christ, but Northrup has pointed out that the gender also shows that the phrase "cannot refer to the coming of Christ . . . for all

the terms used of His coming are feminine in the original" (p. 8). The words he has in mind are such words as *revelation (apokalupsis), coming (parousia),* and *appearing (epiphaneia).*

(3) The strongest proof that "that which is perfect" cannot refer to the Rapture or return of Christ is the plain fact that such an interpretation pointedly contradicts other Scripture passages. According to this interpretation verse 10 says that the gifts of prophecy and knowledge will be terminated when "that which is perfect," understood to mean the Rapture, arrives. Yet there are passages which clearly show that at least the gift of prophecy will again be given by the Holy Spirit after the Rapture. In fact, far from rendering inoperative or terminating the gift of prophecy, the Rapture will initiate a period of unprecedented exercise of the gift! Revelation 11:3-13 describes two major *prophets* who will prophesy during the tribulation and will exhibit powers strikingly similar to those of Moses and Elijah. In the Millennial Age to follow, according to Joel 2:28, the Spirit will be poured out "upon *all* flesh; and your sons and your daughters shall *prophesy,* your old men shall dream dreams, your young men shall see visions."

If these passages in Joel and Revelation are correct, and they must be because they are in God's Word, then the interpretation that "that which is perfect" refers to the Rapture or the Second Coming cannot be correct. These events positively will *not* make the gift of prophecy inoperative; yet Paul stated in A.D. 55 that the partial gifts of prophecy and knowledge *would* be made inoperative by the arrival of "that which is perfect"!

The Canon.—The second, and much more plausible, interpretation understands "that which is perfect" as referring to the completion of the New Testament canon when John penned the Book of Revelation in A.D. 96.

To understand this position it is necessary to carefully examine several aspects of Paul's statements in 1 Corinthians 13:8-13. Three distinctive interpretations are necessary if this view is to be accepted:

(1) Adherents of this interpretation argue that the translation of the Greek word *teleios* as "perfect" is misleading. According to Moulton and Milligan (p. 629) the word has the literal meaning, "having reached its end *(telos)."* It is argued that the primary meaning has reference to the completion of a process. Abbott-Smith suggested the meaning "finished, mature, complete . . . full grown" (p. 442). Paul used the word on two other occasions in 1 Corinthians. In 2:6 the phrase "them that are perfect" refers to mature Christians in contrast to the immature and carnal Corinthians (3:3). In 14:20 the Authorized Version translates this same word "men." Here Paul was really telling the Corinthians that he wished they would stop being immature in their evaluation and use of tongues: "Brethren, be not children in your thinking, but in malice be babies, and in your thinking be *mature."* It is obvious that the word *need not* refer to perfection in the absolute sense and at least in some cases is more properly translated "complete" or "mature."

Based upon this definition it may be argued that the purpose of Paul's statement was to predict that that which was partial, the gifts of prophecy and knowledge, would be rendered inoperative, made unnecessary, when the mature or complete thing arrived. In this case the rendering inoperative of the partial would really be the result of the completion or maturation of the partial. This would mean that when God's revelation for this age was mature, or completed, these partial gifts were not needed for the remainder of the age. "For we know in part and we prophesy in part. But when that which is complete comes, that which is partial shall be rendered inoperative" (1 Cor. 13:9-10).

The statement about knowing "in part" and prophesying "in part" seems to indicate that no one person had the gifts of prophecy and knowledge to such an extent that he understood everything. Paul disclaimed having such comprehensive understanding, even though he probably exercised these gifts to a greater extent than anyone else (13:2). These gifts were shared (Greek, *ek merous,* literally, "out of part") and required supplementation by others with the same gifts, as well as by repeated exercise of these gifts. The view under consideration asserts that "that which is complete" should logically be of the same kind as "that which is partial" and is therefore most naturally understood as a reference to the completion of revelation for the Church Age. This was accomplished in A.D. 96 when the Apostle John wrote the last apostolic epistle. (It should be apparent that either of the other interpretations of "that which is perfect" could also accept the definition of *telios* as referring to the completion or maturation of revelation by means of these gifts— without dating this at the completion of the canon. The "eternal state" view, however, could also accept *telios* as designating the perfect *age* or *state.* The "canon" view cannot allow this possibility.)

(2) If "that which is perfect" designates the completion of the canon, for the sake of consistency in logic, the interpreter must understand verse 12 as referring to a different time. "For now we see in a mirror dimly, but then face to face. Now I know in part, but then I shall know fully even as also I have been fully known." While a few commentators have attempted to explain this verse as also referring to the completion of the Scriptures, such an interpretation certainly offers an inadequate explanation of the phrase "face to face." Even with the completed Word or in the completed Word believers do not see God and spiritual realities "face to face," but "in a mirror

dimly," as Paul implies again in 2 Corinthians 3:18. Also, even today with the completed Scriptures, even the most devout believer does not "know fully" just as also he "was fully known."

If the completion of the canon is in view in verse 10 then one must understand Paul as describing a *process* in verses 8-12. The first stage for the church, during which there were partial revelations, might be compared to infancy. A period of growth leads to maturity. But as with the individual believer, maturity is not the final state, glorification follows; so with the church the period following the completion (maturing) of revelation is not the final state. The final state for the church must include a "face to face" relationship with the Lord when knowledge will be no longer partial or indirect, as in a mirror, but full and direct. Barnes correctly noted that the major emphasis in verse 12 is on a difference in *manner* of knowledge, not just in the extent of knowledge (p. 775).

In this view, verse 10 simply states that the partial gifts involved in revealing church truth will be rendered inoperative by their completion in the New Testament canon. Verse 11 illustrates this as a process of growing up. Verse 12 adds to the argument by emphasizing just how temporary and how partial those present gifts were. It is obvious that they are temporary, Paul said, because in the future we shall know in a completely different manner. Even the completed revelation of the New Testament does not compare with that glory which will be revealed in Him when we see Him face to face. The revelation of God in the person of Jesus will be far greater than even the "mature" revelation in the Word! Even the infallible Word is only a mirror (2 Cor. 3:18)!

(3) One more distinction must be noted before this view can be properly understood. This concerns the meaning of the verb *katargeō*. This verb occurs four times

in verses 8-11 and is translated differently each time in the Authorized Version: "shall fail," "shall vanish away," "shall be done away," and "put away." The basic meaning of the word is to express the idea, "to make inoperative." Representative meanings listed by Delling include, to make "unemployed" or "unused," "to render inactive," "to condemn to inactivity," "to put out of use," "to set aside," "to put out of action," "to take from the sphere of operation" (Kittel, I, 452-54).

It has been suggested that *katargeō* received its meaning by association with darkness or night, "when no man can work" (Moulton and Milligan, p. 331). In modern Greek *arga* means "late." *Katargeō* is an appropriate word for describing the laying aside at darkness of a work which will be resumed the following day. The Biblical word is a combination of three elements: *kata,* "down;" *a,* the negative; and *ergon,* "work." The resultant meanings, "to make inoperative" or "to lay aside," while they do not *require* a later reactivation, clearly allow for such. Only when *katargeō* is used in the perfect tense, as in verse 11, does it, in itself, require that the "laying aside" be permanent. In this case it is not the verbal idea itself but the special significance of the Greek perfect tense, emphasizing the continuing results of an action, which suggests permanence for the "laying aside." In the other tenses the word simply designates a laying aside without any indication as to its duration. Only the context can be determinative as to the presence or absence of a later reactivation.

It should be apparent that this view, understanding "that which is perfect" as the completion of the New Testament, must require that *katargeō* was employed in verses 8 and 10 for the specific reason that it may allow for a later reactivation. Since the gift of prophecy will be given during the tribulation (Rev. 11:3-13) and millennium (Joel 2:28), if one asserts that it was "laid aside" by the completion of the canon he obviously must understand that laying aside as temporary.

The Eternal State.—The view that "that which is perfect" refers to the Rapture was shown to be untenable. The view that this statement refers to the completion of the New Testament canon, while it has not been disproved, has been shown to be based upon several merely plausible or possible considerations. A third alternative is that the eternal state is in view. It seems apparent that many of the older commentaries which were written from a postmillennial or amillennial viewpoint really had in mind the eternal state when they mistakenly identified "that which is perfect" with the "Second Coming." The author is deeply grateful to Dr. Gary Staats, Professor at Multnomah School of the Bible, for providing, in personal correspondence, a fresh and stimulating defense of this interpretation. Two major considerations strongly suggest that this is the correct interpretation:

(1) Probably the strongest factor in favor of understanding "that which is perfect" as referring to the eternal state is that it is the easiest and simplest interpretation. It requires no tenuous exegesis for it merely states that when the eternal state arrives the gifts of prophecy and knowledge will no longer be needed. This simplicity would seem to fit Paul's purpose quite adequately. The context suggests that his purpose was to assert the *fact* of their future cessation, the fact that they are temporal and not eternal, rather than to give a *date* for their cessation.

(2) Also favoring this interpretation are the textual indications that verse 10 and verse 12 are referring to the same time. The phrase, "that which is perfect" (v. 10) is paralleled with "I shall know fully just as also I was fully known" (and indirectly with "face to face," v. 12) by the fact that both are contrasted with that which is "partial."

(The Greek term *ek merous* occurs three times in verses 9 and 10 and once in verse 12.) Since "full knowledge" is said to replace partial knowledge (v. 12), and "that which is perfect" is said to replace partial knowledge (v. 10), it is logical and natural to conclude that "that which is perfect" and "full knowledge" (with its parallel "face to face") must refer to the same thing and time.

It has been demonstrated earlier that the other two interpretations of "that which is perfect" cannot fit with this seemingly simple and logical identification. The "Rapture" view, while properly identifying "that which is perfect" with "face to face" and "full knowledge," commits logical suicide by identifying this event with the rapture, which will *not* terminate the partial gifts. The "canon" view must deny the indentification of "that which is perfect" with "face to face" and "full knowledge" because it is obvious that the completion of the canon did not initiate a "face to face" relationship and "full knowledge."

Another minor consideration concerns a textual variant in verse 10. The Authorized Version reads, "when that which is perfect is come, *then* that which is in part shall be done away." The word "then" *(tote)* does not appear in the modern critical editions of the Greek New Testament. It *is* found, however, in the majority of Greek manuscripts, those of the Byzantine family, as well as in a great number of manuscripts belonging to other textual families. *If* it should be found to be authentic this would certainly favor identifying the time of the "then" in verse 12 with the time of the "then" in verse 10.

Tongues cease before prophecies

As indicated earlier, tongues advocates commonly identify "that which is perfect" with an event which terminates this age or introduces the millennium and then conclude that 1 Corinthians 13:8-10 states that tongues are to remain until that event. It has been demonstrated that their identification of "that which is perfect" is fallacious. It may also be clearly demonstrated that no matter how one may define "that which is perfect," neither this passage nor any other suggests that tongues were to continue until that event or state. The following considerations will substantiate this statement.

(1) In this regard, the most important textual detail is that tongues are *not* named among those gifts which are said to be made inoperative by the arrival of "that which is perfect." To repeat, the passage only states that the revelatory gifts, the gifts which impart knowledge, specifically the gifts of prophecy and knowledge, would be made inoperative by the arrival of "that which is perfect." In the eternal state such gifts will be unnecessary because *all* believers will have a full knowledge and a "face to face" relationship with Christ. The fact that tongues are *not* named among those gifts which will become inoperative at that time certainly allows for, if it does not require, their *prior* cessation. In view of their purpose, one may conclude that the passage *requires* such prior cessation.

(2) The Holy Spirit also in another way places tongues in a different category from those gifts which will become inoperative when "that which is perfect" arrives. He does so by employing a different verb and a different voice with tongues. The verb employed with prophecy and knowledge, *katargeō,* has been examined earlier. It means to "lay aside," or "render inoperative," either temporarily or permanently as required by the context. The "canon" view requires it to mean a temporary setting aside. The "eternal state" view requires it to mean a permanent setting aside. As seen above, the latter is the easiest and most natural interpretation.

For some reason, Paul and the Holy Spirit chose not to use *katargeō* in the statement about tongues. Right *between* two uses of this verb with the other gifts the statement about tongues is inserted and a different verb is employed. The verb that is used with tongues, *pauō*, simply means "to stop" or "cease." In his scholarly study of this verb, Dungey concluded that it has the "intrinsic idea of voluntary or natural cessation because of the nature of the activity or because of the will of the individual doing the action" (p. 21).

Perhaps more important than the change of verbs is the change of voice. The three occurrences of *katargeō* in verses 8-10 are all in the passive voice. This means that the gifts of prophecy and knowledge will *be* made inoperative (acted upon) and the implication of verses 10-12 is that that which will render them inoperative is the arrival of "that which is perfect" or full, "face to face" knowledge. But this is not the case with tongues. It is not said that tongues will *be* rendered inoperative, but merely that they will stop or cease. The verb *pauō* is not in the passive, but in the middle voice. (Greek has an active and a passive voice like English, but also a "middle" voice.)

The exact significance of the middle voice here has been the subject of considerable debate. The function of the middle voice normally is to intensify the part that the subject plays in the action. The famous *Grammar* by Dana and Mantey lists this verb as an illustration of an "intensive" or "dynamic" middle. They conclude that the Greeks employed the middle in such cases where in English "we must resort to italics" (p. 155). This would mean that the most emphatic statement in the context—placed *between* the statements about prophecy and knowledge—is the statement, *"tongues . . . shall cease."*

It is probably better, however, to understand this verb as an intransitive deponent middle with an active meaning. The verb is normally intransitive in the middle (or employs. a complimentary participle). (The only active form in the New Testament, in 1 Peter 3:10, is transitive.) It is significant that the Septuagint uses the verb *pauō* in the middle voice fifteen times to translate the Hebrew word which means "to be complete, at an end, finished, accomplished, spent" (Brown, Driver, and Briggs, pp. 477-78). The great lexicon by Liddell and Scott says that in the middle *pauō* denotes a *"willing,"* or one would assume, a *natural,* cessation—whereas in the passive it denotes a *"forced"* cessation (p. 1350). This fits well with all that has been seen above. Tongues will not be *forced* out of existence, nor be terminated or replaced by the arrival of "that which is perfect" or the full knowledge of the eternal state. On the contrary, rather than being put out of existence by any eschatological event, they will simply *stop* or *cease* in the natural process of things. Their *purpose* places this cessation within the Apostolic Age.

(3) Though "that which is perfect" is accepted as designating the eternal state, the passage does not require that even the gifts of prophecy and knowledge must continue in operation throughout the Church Age. Ephesians 2:20 specifically states that the apostles and prophets belong to the foundational stage of the church. Since an apostle was one who had been personally commissioned by the risen Lord this foundational stage is clearly limited to the generation of those individuals. And since Ephesians 2:20 so closely links the apostles and prophets one may readily affirm that *as far as the Church Age is concerned* the gift of prophecy was limited to the foundational stage. This does not deny its later appearance *after* the Church Age and prior to the inauguration of the eternal state.

(4) The argument of 1 Corinthians 13:8-10 is illustra-

ted in verse 11 by Paul's analogy with physical growth. "When I was a baby, I used to *speak* as a baby, used to *think* as a baby, used to *reason* as a baby. But when I have become a man I have put away the baby things."

In the Authorized Version the last clause is translated, "But *when I became* a man, I put away childish things." This implies that at the moment of reaching maturity, a man simultaneously puts away all the things of infancy. This is obviously not true and the Greek text does not suggest it. With two verbs in the perfect tense, the sense is, "By the time when I have become a man, I *have put away* the things of infancy."

Everyone knows that the things of infancy are not put away all at one time, but are gradually and successively put away during growth toward maturity. One of the first things to go is baby talk. A child's vocabulary is always ahead of his comprehension. He readily learns and repeats words, but often with little concept of their proper meaning. After his baby talk has ceased, the child's thinking and reasoning continue to mature. By the time he reaches maturity, he has permanently put away babyish speaking, thinking, and reasoning.

Some scholars believe that Paul's reference to *three* characteristics of infancy, rather than two or four, is not just accidental. They see a correspondence between these three aspects of infancy and the three gifts under discussion (Godet, II, 252-53). The illustration of growth does not favor a simultaneous putting away of all the things of infancy. Quite the opposite is true. If the reference to babyish speaking is in any way paralleled with the gift of tongues, as many have assumed, then the implication is that like baby talk, tongues would be the first to disappear. Whether or not this analogy was intended by the Spirit, the illustration certainly allows for the possibility of some things being laid aside before others.

(5) One final consideration harmonizes well with the Biblical evidence requiring the cessation of tongues prior to the cessation of the other two gifts. The purpose of the other two gifts was primarily revelatory. Also, the gifts of prophecy and knowledge are by no means limited to the Church Age. (Though it has been shown that as far as the Church Age is concerned they were limited to the foundational stage.) These two gifts were given during the Old Testament period (Deut. 18:15, Dan. 1:17, Ex. 31:3) and will also be given during the tribulation (Rev. 11:3) and millennium (Joel 2:28, Jer. 31:34). But, as has been seen, tongues were not revelational. There is no proof that the Holy Spirit has caused them or will cause them in any but the Church Age. As far as revelation is concerned they are connected only with the foundational stage of the church. They were intended to serve as *signs* (Mk. 16:17) in authenticating the apostles' ministry.

In Summary

(1) Three views concerning the identity of "that which is perfect" have been outlined. The "Rapture" view has been rejected. The "completion of the canon" view, while it has not been absolutely disproved requires several tenuous suppositions. The "eternal state" view allows the simplest and most natural understanding of the passage.

(2) In 1 Corinthians 13:9 and 10 Paul simply states that the partial gifts of prophecy and knowledge will be made unnecessary, rendered inoperative, by the arrival of the eternal state.

(3) Though these revelatory gifts will be exercised in the tribulation and millennium, the passage does not say that they will continue to be exercised throughout the whole Church Age. This is, in fact, specifically denied by the fact that *as far as the church is concerned* prophecy is linked with apostleship as belonging to the foundational stage of the church (Eph. 2:20).

(4) The gift of tongues is not said to be replaced or finally terminated by the arrival of "that which is perfect" as are the other two gifts. This, along with an understanding of their purpose and the simple prediction that they *would* cease, *requires* the cessation of tongues at a time prior to the termination of the other two gifts—namely within the Apostolic Age.

Tongues Ceased

On the basis of exegesis it has been concluded that Spirit-caused tongues came to an end during the Apostolic Age. This is also substantiated by historical evidence. Since the text gives no hint of successive or repeated reactivations it is natural to assume that when they ceased, they ceased, never to be reactivated. Historical evidence demands that the cessation of tongues be placed within the Apostolic Age.

The Apostolic Fathers

After a thorough study of the writings of these church leaders of the generation immediately succeeding the apostles, Rogers wrote, "It is significant that the gift is nowhere alluded to, hinted at, or found in the Apostolic Fathers" (p. 134). As Rogers has shown, this silence of the Apostolic Fathers should not be passed off as merely an argument from silence. The evidence cited by Rogers involves four considerations.

(1) A primary consideration is the fact that these Fathers addressed churches where tongues speaking had occurred according to the Biblical record. For example, Clement of Rome wrote to the Corinthians about A.D. 95 and discussed their spiritual problems but did not mention tongues. The Holy Spirit had stopped giving the gift, and as a result of Paul's letter the Corinthians had apparently also stopped misusing the ability originally granted to them by God. Tongues had lost their prestige

since Paul had pointed out the carnality of the Corinthians and had shown that their use of tongues was an indication of spiritual immaturity.

(2) A second significant factor is the widespread geographical coverage of these Fathers. They represented and wrote to practically every area of the Roman Empire. If Christians had been speaking in tongues, certainly one of the Fathers would have mentioned it.

(3) Also, the writings of these Fathers were strongly doctrinal. They discussed practically every major doctrine of the New Testament, yet did not mention tongues. Obviously they did not consider tongues important for the normal Christian experience.

(4) Finally, the purpose of their writings should be considered. They wrote to explain Christianity, to correct Christians, to defend Christianity, and to show the superiority of Christianity over Judaism and other religions— yet they did not mention tongues.

After studying the historical evidence, Warfield concluded that "the possession of the charismata was confined to the Apostolic Age" (p. 6). It may be affirmed that the generation which immediately succeeded the apostles did not consider tongues an experience to be desired by all Christians. Like the other unusual manifestations of the Spirit, tongues were understood as an authenticating sign accompanying the apostolic ministry.

Later leaders

Justin Martyr.—The learned Justin (c. 100-165) traveled widely throughout the Roman Empire. If tongues were practiced among devout believers he would have known of it. His extensive writings in defense of Christianity never mentioned tongues. In arguing for the superiority of Christianity over Judaism he mentioned spiritual gifts and listed those he had in mind: gifts of understanding, counsel, strength, healing, foreknowledge, teaching, and the fear of God (Rogers, pp. 136-38).

Montanus.—A pagan priest named Montanus was converted to Christianity about A.D. 150. He and his prophetesses spoke in tongues. However, the facts that his doctrine contradicted the Scriptures and his prophecies proved false (see Chapter One) prove that his tongues were not caused by the Holy Spirit.

Irenaeus.—Tongues advocates consider the testimony of Irenaeus (c. 140-203) an outstanding proof that tongues continued to occur in the early centuries of church history. "We have heard," he reported, that many brethren have prophetic gifts and "through the Spirit of God do speak in all kinds of languages." In evaluating this statement several considerations should be pointed out. (1) Irenaeus had been influenced by the Montanists and had even carried an appeal to Rome for kindly treatment of them. (2) He himself did not speak in tongues, and apparently none of his associates at Lyons did, for he used the plural "we have heard." (3) In writing about the events at Pentecost, he gave no hint that the experience was operative in his time. (See Roberts, Vol. I: *Against Heresies*; III, 12; V. 61.)

Since he only said that he had heard of tongues it is proper to conclude that he did not consider them an essential or even as a normative element of Christian experience (Rogers, pp. 138-40).

Tertullian.—Around A.D. 202 Tertullian (c. 150-222) was converted to Montanism so it is not surprising that he alluded to tongues. The surprising fact is that he only made two such allusions! Some scholars think that one of these refers to the signs associated with the apostles rather than to contemporary signs. In writings on 1

Corinthians 12-14 he did not mention any gifts in his day!

The only clear statement about contemporary tongues in his writings refers to one of the Montanist prophetesses who "in an ecstasy of the spirit . . . converses with angels, and, sometimes with the Lord Himself." He obviously viewed this lady as an exceptional case.

According to Gromacki, apparently Tertullian eventually "became disenchanted with the pneumatic excesses of the Montanists" and separated from them (p. 14). The important thing about Tertullian's testimony is that *this is the last witness to contemporary tongues speaking in the writings of the Church Fathers. This means that there is no reported occurrence of tongues speaking after the apostles in any writings of the Church Fathers except for the instances cited, which are all allusions to the practice among the Montanists!*

Origen.—Origen (c. 185-253) is recognized as one of the most scholarly men of his day. He read and traveled extensively, and students from all over the world attended his classes. If tongues had been known or expected in his day he would have known it; yet in all his voluminous writing he never referred to tongues as a contemporary phenomenon. In his apologetic against Celsus he explicitly argued that the signs of the Apostolic Age had been temporary and that no contemporary Christians exercised any of the ancient prophetical gifts. Kelsey, though he looks with favor on tongues, reported that from Origen on the references to tongues by the Church Fathers are mostly "explanations as to why the phenomena which had occurred in Biblical times were no longer occurring" (p. 39).

Chrysostom.—Schaff said of Chrysostom (347-407), "No one of the Oriental fathers has left a more spotless reputation; no one is so much read and so often quoted by modern commentators" (III, 933-34). In commenting on the 1 Corinthians tongues passage, Chrysostom confessed, "This whole place is very obscure: but the obscurity is produced by our ignorance of the facts referred to and by their cessation, being such as then used to occur, but now no longer take place" (*Homilies,* XXIX, 1).

Augustine.—Undoubtedly the greatest theologian among all the Church Fathers was Augustine (354-430). In commenting on Acts 2:4 he said, "In the earliest times, 'the Holy Ghost fell upon them that believed: and they spake with tongues.' . . . These were signs adapted to the time. For there behooved to be that betokening of the Holy Spirit. . . . That thing was done for a betokening, and it passed away" (*Homilies on First John,* VI, 10).

In another work he stated that "in former days" the Holy Spirit had been given by the laying on of hands, "amid the testimony of temporal sensible miracles" in association with the "rudimentary faith" and "the first beginnings of the church." He made it clear that no one expected such things in his day (*On Baptism,* III, 16).

The greatest Church Fathers of the East and the West considered tongues a remote practice associated only with the Apostolic Age. Chrysostom clearly stated that tongues were so remote that the nature of the gift as it was demonstrated in the Apostolic Age was unknown to Christians in the fourth and fifth centuries.

Conclusion

In this chapter it has been demonstrated that the gift of tongues was limited in duration by its purpose, which was to authenticate the authority of the apostles and consequently their message. If the unusual manifestations of the Spirit's presence and power were intended for all believers of the whole Church Age, how could they have served as "the signs of an apostle"?

It was also seen that 1 Corinthians 13 intimates that tongues would go out of existence before the two other gifts would be finally terminated. Though it is often so interpreted, this passage does *not* say that tongues are supposed to continue until "that which is perfect."

Lastly, the testimony of history was presented as in agreement with the above conclusions. Tongues were not practiced by orthodox Christians for many centuries following the Apostolic Age. The testimony of the fathers is that the "thing was done for a betokening, and it passed away." It is concluded that since the Apostolic Age the Holy Spirit has not and will not again cause people to speak in tongues.

Paul closes his argument concerning the temporary nature of the three gifts he has mentioned by contrasting them with three *enduring* things: "And now, in conclusion, there are three things which stay and are permanent. Faith abides, hope abides, love abides. These three are permanent. But of these the greatest is love" (1 Cor. 13:13, interpretative paraphrase by Boyer, p. 124).

By saying "these three," he was obviously drawing a sharp contrast with *those three. These* three are abiding; *those* three are not.

CHAPTER 5

The Psychology of Tongues and the Modern Phenomenon

In order to understand the modern tongues movement and counsel those who are being influenced by it, it is necessary (1) to examine the characteristics of the modern phenomenon and then (2) to evaluate the psychological factors that have been suggested as accompanying or explaining it.

Characteristics of the Modern Phenomenon

The purpose of this section is to evaluate briefly several of the most significant factors regarding the practice of tongues speaking as it appears in the modern "charismatic revival." The factors to be considered are: (1) the nature of the tongues utterances, (2) the absence of spontaneity, (3) the disillusionment which often follows in the wake of tongues, (4) the exercise of the "gift of interpretation," and (5) the ignoring of the Scriptural injunctions regarding tongues.

The nature of the tongues

Tongues speakers themselves do not agree on the nature of their gift. Some consider their tongues as real

93

human languages which are just normally not recognized either by the speaker or by his audience. Others view them as not being any language normally used by human beings, but nevertheless as a "language" in the sense that they are reducible to writing. Probably the majority of tongues speakers properly understand their "unknown tongues" as unintelligible utterances, not a language employed by any group of persons and not characterized by any system of specific sound-symbols.

What are the facts regarding the nature of modern tongues? It is often stated that certain individuals have delivered a clear message or even preached the gospel in a language they have never heard. Some have undoubtedly convinced themselves that this has happened; however, under careful examination their conviction often wavers, and there is always considerable room for doubt. There seems to be no positive and unassailable evidence that anyone has ever presented the gospel in an unlearned language. Numerous psychologists and linguists have listened to hundreds of tongues utterances and evaluated many hours of tongues recordings, but no recorded instance of religious tongues speech has ever contained a clear message in any language. A group of government linguists found tongues to be unrecognizable (Farrell, p. 203).

Dr. Kenneth Pike, the famous linguist with the University of Michigan, frequently amazes his audience with a demonstration in which within about fifteen minutes he is able to converse in simple sentences with a person whose language he has never heard before. Experts with such ability have evaluated tongues recordings for days and have concluded that they cannot be considered as language in the sense of conveying thought (Burdick, pp. 60-61; Bergsma, p. 10). Eugene Nida, the renowned linguist with the American Bible Society, conducted an analysis of tongues recorded on tape. He was assisted by specialists representing more than 150 aboriginal languages in twenty-five different countries. He concluded that tongues bear no resemblance to any actual language ever treated by linguists (Mills, p. 11). He described them as a form of ecstatic speech, similar to that which occurs all over the world in many religious practices, wherein one's own inventory of sounds is employed in nonsense combinations, but with simulated "foreign" or exotic features (Gromacki, p. 67).

One of the most thorough linguistic evaluations of tongues was conducted by William Samarin. He concluded that the major features of tongues speech are that it "consists of strings of generally simple syllables" which "are not matched systematically with a semantic system," and are consequently "lexically meaningless" (pp. 127, 211).

The absence of spontaneity

Advocates of tongues often refer to the "charismatic revival" as a spontaneous revival accomplished solely by the sovereign work of the Holy Spirit. It may be responded that if there is one thing the "charismatic revival" cannot claim it is spontaneity.

Few religious movements have been promoted with such coordination of effort and expenditure of funds for publicity. The Full Gospel Business Men's Fellowship International, headed by the wealthy Shakarian family, is only one of the many national and global organizations supporting this "revival" by the most polished of public relations techniques. Oral Roberts University and other educational institutions are helping to make this experience respectable all over the world. *Christian Life,* as well as many denominationally and individually sponsored magazines, have been propagandizing for tongues for years. Leading national magazines have carried articles on the movement and on individuals in it. Books by denominational leaders such as Kelsey and Christenson and widely publicized books such as Sherrill's *They Speak With Other Tongues* have helped to make tongues respectable.

Another proof that the "charismatic revival" should not be considered a spontaneous revival is the fact that tongues speakers have had to be coached, coaxed, and forced into their utterances. Tongues speaking is definitely a *learned* skill (Kildahl, p. 74). Promoters of tongues present formulas and instructions designed to teach interested parties how to speak in tongues. Almost invariably these instructions include a prescription to begin by making sounds of some kind, such as by repetition of a phrase, or by determining to utter sounds that include no known words.

Christenson, for example, presents speaking in tongues as an act of faith. It is something which you must knowingly begin, he says, and trust that God will continue (pp. 125-27). He grants that persons are coaxed and coached into speaking in tongues but argues that the continuation of this exercise is a gift of the Spirit. "Precisely how a person begins speaking in tongues is not as important as how he continues to use the gift day by day," he asserts (p. 127).

Such "logic" is certainly illogical. Christenson himself states that "once a person has spoken in tongues, he may do so at will thereafter" (pp. 130-31). (It is something like riding a bicycle. Once learned, it is repeatable.) Yet the Biblical example of the Corinthians is quite instructive. Here was a case where the Holy Spirit had caused their original tongues speaking; that is, He had given them the gift; yet they were misusing this ability on later occasions. If those whom the Holy Spirit had originally caused to speak in tongues could later misuse that ability, it is illogical to say that one who *caused himself* to speak in tongues may be assured that his *continued* use of tongues is under the Spirit's direction!

It is almost inconceivable that an ability secured by such intensive self-effort could be considered a proof of anything, much less a sovereign gift of the Spirit who distributes gifts "to each one individually just as He purposes" (1 Cor. 12:11). Reports of individuals spontaneously speaking in tongues are exceedingly rare (Samarin, pp. 51-52). It would be difficult to prove that Christians today ever do so apart from some preconceptions about tongues. Whatever may be claimed for the modern movement, it cannot be called a spontaneous revival.

Disillusionment

Since modern tongues are deliberately initiated by the tongues speakers themselves, it is no wonder that many soon become disillusioned with their experience. It often appears that the more sincere the believer, the more severe the disillusionment. Though it is understandably difficult for one who has espoused this experience to admit that it has not brought—or, in his mind, no longer brings—the expected blessings, many have been honest enough to admit this. Leaders of the charismatic movement are aware of this problem and often offer suggestions for dealing with this disappointment.

Christenson warns neophites that "two 'testings' of this gift seem *almost universal,*" and suggests that "a word concerning them may save those who are new in the gift some needless anxiety" (p. 131, emphasis mine).

Artificiality.—The first temptation Christenson cites is the temptation to think, "I am just making this up." He admits that this is a natural temptation but urges that it be repelled with all vigor. This amounts to a patent admission that one's common sense tells him that an ability so "worked up" is not a work of the Spirit. Tongues speakers usually respond that the gift cannot be artificial because the tongues speaker has asked God for a spiritual gift, and, after all, if one asks God for bread, will he be given a stone (Mt. 7:9)? The answer, of course, is that the "gift" was not received from God.

Ineffectuality.—The second temptation usually comes after one has been exercising the gift for some time—after the initial joy and enthusiasm have dimmed. The tongues speaker may begin to feel that the gift is no longer "doing anything" for him and consequently he often neglects it or allows it to fall into disuse. Christenson suggests that every gift of God involves a stewardship and therefore one must resolve to use it all the rest of his life. This amounts to saying that the "gift," which was *sought* and begun by artificial means, must be continued at all cost, even when common sense says it is a hollow mockery. Again it should be remembered that the rationale given to support such a charade is simply that there *was* a gift of tongues in the Apostolic Age, and therefore this is an experience to be desired by every believer!

Disaffectation.—There is perhaps a third consideration regarding those who become disillusioned with tongues. Kildahl and Qualben, following psychological testing of tongues speakers, asserted that when tongues are an important life goal there is always a relationship to a leader or a group which conveys a feeling of acceptance and belonging. A crucial factor for those who stop the practice of speaking in tongues, they said, is the loss of confidence in the authority figure who introduced them to the experience (pp. 53, 79-81).

This consideration may obviously be linked with the two which precede it. If one should conclude that his tongues are artificial or ineffectual he might readily lose respect for the person(s) who introduced him to tongues, or even for all who speak in tongues. Contrariwise, one who is losing respect for his tongues leader might be expected to doubt the reality and value of the experience. Kildahl stated that he and Qualben "found no tongue-speaker who was unrelated to a glossolalia authority figure whom he esteemed" (p. 80). This broad statement undoubtedly indicates a limited contact with tongues speakers; however, this dependence upon an authority figure does seem to be a significant consideration, especially among traditional Pentecostal groups.

The modern "gift of interpretation"

In every case where a claim to have the gift of interpretation of tongues has been weighed, it has been found wanting. Scientific analysis has pointed out that there is no relationship between the tongues and the supposed interpretation. A few "words" may be interpreted by many sentences, and vice versa. The same sounds may be recorded and interpreted differently by each "interpreter," or the same interpreter may explain the same sounds differently on different occasions (Kildahl, p. 63).

S. E. Polivina reported an incident when John 3:3 was recited in the Austrian language, but the interpreter claimed that Acts 19:2 had been recited in French (Bell, pp. 71-72)! A young seminarian in Dallas memorized the Twenty-Third Psalm in Hebrew and recited it in a tongues service. The interpreter's explanation was entirely unrelated to the Psalm.

The supposed "revelations" given by interpreters are usually vapid and meaningless. Sometimes they contradict the clear teaching of the Word. (The same may be said for the "prophecies" given by those professing to have the gift of prophecy.)

Scriptural injunctions ignored

Even during the period when the Holy Spirit occasion-ally caused people to speak in tongues, restrictions be-came necessary because of misuse. Against that which is truly caused by the Spirit "there is no law" (Gal. 5:23). Along with all else that Paul said on the subject, the limitations he placed upon tongues were so restrictive that they quickly disappeared from the Corinthian con-gregation. The Holy Spirit ceased causing the experience (1 Cor. 13:8), and because Paul removed its prestige value and circumscribed its usage, the Corinthians stopped mis-using it. Four major restrictions are enumerated in 1 Corinthians 14:26-40.

The number.—No more than three should ever speak in tongues at any meeting, and preferably no more than two (v. 27). Even this was a concession. "If anyone speaks" ("should speak"), means, "In spite of what I have said—that in an assembly I had rather speak five understand-able words than myriads of words in tongues—if anyone still thinks he must speak, let him at least observe these restrictions."

The order.—Those who did speak in tongues were re-quired to do so "by course," that is, one at a time (v. 27).

The interpretation.—When no one present had the gift of interpretation, all the tongues speakers were to remain silent (v. 28). The common English translation, "Let him keep silence in the church," has led many neo-Pentecostal groups to boast that they will not publicly use tongues in a "church" service, but only in "cottage" or home prayer meetings. The Corinthians, however, did not have a "church" building, and Paul's statement should read, "Let him be silent in an assembly." The Greek has no arti-cle and the statement refers to any gathering of believers.

The prohibition.—Women were not permitted to speak

in tongues in any assembly of believers. "Let the women be silent in the assemblies," Paul said (vv. 34-36). No matter how one may wish otherwise to limit or expand this statement, it has *particular* reference to tongues and prophesying. It is interesting that the Pentecostal movement was begun by the tongues speaking of a woman, Agnes Ozman. Women have often gained prominence in the movement. Samarin remarks that "one of the things that glossolalia does for women . . . is to give them a greater share in an institution that is dominated traditionally by men" (p. 223). Stegall estimated that at least 85 percent of the persons who have spoken in tongues in traditional Pentecostal assemblies are women (p. 36). Samarin estimates that in neo-Pentecostalism there is a fairly even balance of men and women (p. 224).

Obviously, some tongues speakers attempt to restrict their use of tongues in accordance with Paul's injunctions. But this does not prove that theirs is a genuine gift of the Spirit. It has been established in the preceding chapters that the Holy Spirit only gave the gift of tongues during the Apostolic Age. The purpose of outlining these restrictions is simply to show that even if the gift were given by the Spirit today, the "charismatic revival" as a whole would be guilty of misusing the gift, for both the "old" Pentecostals and the neo-Pentecostals are often guilty of violating Paul's restrictions.

Psychological Considerations Regarding Modern Tongues

In evaluating the experience of tongues as it occurs today, it is necessary to answer three questions. (1) What is the source of these tongues? (2) What are the psychological explanations? (3) What is the cause of the present interest in tongues?

What is the source of tongues?

The Holy Spirit.—Christian tongues speakers, of

course, insist that the Holy Spirit is responsible for the modern movement. At the same time, however, many sincere Pentecostal ministers will grant that some of their members only pretend to receive the gift, and many who really do speak in tongues give no evidence of any genuine work of the Spirit in their lives. As indicated in Chapter I, the fact that even the most ardent tongues advocate must admit that tongues speaking is not proof *per se* of the Holy Spirit's presence undermines the whole charismatic movement. If *some* of it is not of God, how can it be asserted that any particular manifestation is a result of the Spirit's work?

Demons.—Some Christians, having rightly concluded that God is not causing people to speak in tongues, have suggested that all of the present-day tongues speaking is due to satanic or demonic influence. Very few, regardless of their convictions about the validity of tongues, would deny that demon possession is the source of *some* tongues utterances. If tongues are to be explained supernaturally, then they must be either divinely or demonically caused.

Human nature.—Stegall remarked that "there is another source for seeming supernatural phenomenon and that is the merely psychic. It is in the psychic and psychological spheres that all of Pentecostalism and most of Spiritism activities fall" (p. 38). Scroggie also concluded that tongues are largely to be explained as "psychical rather than spiritual in nature" (1919, p. 19).

Evaluation.—The preceding chapters have shown that God granted the gift of tongues in the Apostolic Age for a purpose which no longer exists. The Scriptures specifically indicate that the Holy Spirit ceased causing the gift during the Apostolic Age. Consequently, though tongues may be a genuine "religious" experience, even among sincere Christians, *no* occurrence of modern tongues is produced by the Holy Spirit.

Again it is admitted even by tongues advocates that "Demon Possession can be a cause" for tongues speaking (Dalton, p. 116). It has been demonstrated, though, and will be further substantiated, that tongues need not be considered as essentially supernatural or miraculous. This means that the Holy Spirit caused individuals to speak in tongues on several occasions in the Apostolic Age, demonic spirits have often caused such utterances, but the experience has most often occurred apart from any "outside" or supernatural causation. While it is not proper to conclude that every person who speaks in tongues is demon possessed, it should be apparent from the preceding considerations that the *movement* is definitely satanically and demonically sponsored.

Ruble pointed to several advantages which accrue to Satan as a result of the modern tongues speaking. "The satanic is mistaken for the divine; the carnal is mistaken for the spiritual; the nonbiblical is mistaken for the biblical; pride is mistaken for humility; emotionalism is mistaken for power; in short error is mistaken for truth. Certainly Satan rejoices in all such mistaken identity. In light of the fact that the present tongues movement has no scriptural basis, it is obviously not of God. If it is not of God, then . . . it must be of Satan. It does not soften the indictment to say that it merely arises out of man's constitution. Satan has access to this, too" (p. 195).

Tongues may be understood as a purely psychological experience. This means that it is not necessary to look for a direct supernatural causation. Tongues speakers are doctrinally confused, but their speaking is not normally a result of demon possession. If a tongues speaker is truly a believer, he should be loved as such and counseled regarding his errors. One's attitude toward a sincere Christian involved in tongues should be like his attitude toward a sincere Christian involved in such a cult as Seventh Day Adventism. The believer in either case may hold to many truths as taught in the Word but also hold certain doctrinal errors traditional to his group.

Though demons are undoubtedly active in the propagation of any false doctrine, it is no more necessary to accuse all tongues speakers of speaking under direct demonic influence than it is to accuse all the adherents of any other doctrinal aberration of such influence. Tongues speaking is a purely psychological possibility available to any human being. "No special power needs to take over a person's vocal organs; all of us are equipped with everything we need to produce glossolalia" (Samarin, p. 211).

For most tongues speakers the problem is not demon possession, but the doctrinal error which led to their seeking such an experience, and the misinterpretation of its significance. Only a Spirit-directed submission to the teaching of the Word can correct such error (1 Cor. 14:37-39).

What are the psychological explanations?

No attempt will be made to list or evaluate all the psychological explanations that have been offered to account for tongues; nor will any attempt be made to *explain* tongues from a psychiatric or medical viewpoint. Such an attempt would be much like trying to explain why one may weep uncontrollably, or how one remembers facts, or how one dreams. The sole assertion here is that tongues *are* a psychological phenomenon. Only a few of the more significant psychological factors will be briefly cited and evaluated where necessary.

A motor automatism.—Many who have written on tongues have suggested that they involve a motor automatism. This is an attempted explanation not of the cause of tongues, but of their nature. Bloesch, for example, has stated that tongues are "a motor automatism which results from a radical inward detachment from one's conscious surroundings. It involves the massive dissociation of all or nearly all voluntary muscles from conscious control. . . . As an automatism tongues are similar to automatic writing, ecstatic jerking, "spirit dancing," and uncontrollable laughter" (pp. 371-72).

Similarly, Burdick refers to tongues as an "abnormal psychological occurrence" in the sense that the brain "is not functioning according to its normal pattern" (pp. 75, 79).

Some writers have referred to tongues as a type of somnambulism. They are conceived of as involving a trancelike state analogous to dreams and visions wherein the unconscious is allowed to take control (Bloesch, p. 373). Since tongues are not a normal experience for most people, it is not surprising that terms such as hysteria, partial catalepsy, neurosis, and similar expressions frequently occur in discussions of this subject (Bergsma, pp. 14-17).

Oates has stated that tongues involve a motor automatism resulting from a form of dissociation within the personality in which certain voluntary muscles are operated by control centers other than those associated with normal consciousness (p. 93).

Though he is aware that dissociation or trancelike tongues are not uncommon in traditional Pentecostalism, since they are rare in neo-Pentecostalism, Samarin feels that it is wise to abandon terms such as "automatic," and "involuntary" when describing tongues (pp. 26, 220). It is true that contemporary charismatists who are proficient (practiced) in their use of tongues are usually well aware of all activities going on around them and are able even to continue routine activities themselves while speaking in tongues. But since the speaker's mind does not consciously select sounds for their *meaning*, perhaps the words "dissociation" and "automatic" will not be misleading as long as it is recognized that a trance or compulsive involuntary behavior is not necessary.

Ecstasy.—Though "ecstasy" is not a technical scientific or psychological term, it often appears in discussions about tongues. It may be variously defined but always includes the concept of emotional excitation. Samarin defines it "simply as a pleasurable state of intense emotion whether natural or linked with an altered state of consciousness" (p. 203). Cutten concluded that all modern tongues "may be classed as ecstasy or allied phenomena" (p. 157).

Probably all writers on this subject would agree that ecstasy is sometimes or usually involved in tongues speech. A few persons who have practiced tongues speaking for years, apparently in an attempt to thwart the charge of excess emotionalism, boast that "one does not have to turn an emotional hair to speak in tongues" (Kelsey, p. 145). It is difficult to understand how one who makes such a statement could consider tongues as either psychologically or spiritually beneficial. It would seem that in order to be reckoned as a part of genuine *worship,* tongues must arise from an extraordinary emotional experience. When they occur apart from emotion, they certainly cannot be considered as in *any* way beneficial, for in such cases *both* the mind *and* the "spirit" are unfruitful (1 Cor. 14:14).

One's understanding of the term "ecstasy" will determine its relevance to tongues. If it is understood as involving involuntary behavior, it is only rarely applicable to tongues. If it is understood only as describing a very strong or unusual emotion, then it is *often* applicable to tongues. In some cases the term is obviously not appropriate at all. When tongues are called "ecstatic utterances" or "languages of ecstasy," these terms are technically applicable only to *most* tongues and are often employed only to distinguish them from normal or semantically controlled speech.

Hypnosis.—Due to the repeated suggestions as to what is expected of one, and the repeated appeals to "yield oneself" to the "power," many writers have concluded that hypnotism is frequently involved in causing tongues. Bloesch remarks, "There is no doubt that both self and group suggestion play some role in this phenomenon. . . . The fact that speaking in tongues is a contagious phenomenon is another evidence of the influence of suggestion. It is something that has to be caught. . . . In this respect it resembles the 'barking' and 'jerking' which occurred in the Kentucky revivals in which thousands were caught up into ecstasy even against their wills" (p. 372). Matthews adds that "In some places the very laws relating to mind reading, telepathy, and hypnosis are followed almost perfectly" (pp. 97-98). Burdick suggests that some who begin to speak in tongues in private may do so as a result of autohypnosis or autosuggestion (p. 70).

John Kildahl, a clinical psychologist, and Paul Qualben, a psychiatrist, after several years of study financed by the American Lutheran Church and the National Institute of Mental Health, concluded that "hypnotizability constitutes the *sine qua non* of the glossolalia experience" (Kildahl, p. 54). "While glossolalia is not the same as hypnosis, it is similar to it and has the same roots in the relationship of the subject to the authority figure" (p. 55). The battery of psychological tests administered by Kildahl and Qualben was interpreted as revealing that tongues speakers are more submissive, suggestible, and dependent upon a leader than those who do not speak in tongues (pp. 38-56). According to Kildahl, this study produced "conclusive evidence" that the benefits reported by tongues speakers are dependent upon acceptance by the leader and other members of the group, and upon their evaluation of the significance of the experience, rather than upon the actual experience itself (p. 55).

A major problem with this view is that "hypnotizability" may vary with time, attitude, instruction, and other factors. Samarin is correct in objecting that a certain type of personality is not required in order for one to speak in tongues, though it is undoubtedly true that "people of a certain type are *attracted* to the kind of religion that uses tongues" (p. 228).

It is probable that a hypnotic effect does contribute to many occurrences of tongues, though apparently not to all. Obviously, this was not the case with the tongues which were initiated by the Holy Spirit in the Apostolic Age.

Psychic catharsis.—Ira Jay Martin viewed tongues as a form of psychic catharsis, a "purging of the soul," which is a genuine, though not universal, concomitant of the Christian conversion experience. He explained that when an individual's personality is radically altered by new religious convictions, sometimes "the psychological upheaval is too great to control; the resultant joy of release from guilt-feeling" gives one a new outlook on life (p. 100).

Obviously, such an explanation could specifically apply only to the *first* occasion of a person's tongues speaking. For this reason Martin labeled such tongues as "genuine" and all later repetitions as "synthetic." These "synthetic" tongues he explained as resulting from "auto-hypnotism, normal hypnosis, and the laws of auto-suggestion stimulating the individual into action" (p. 100).

It is readily granted that tongues have sometimes been followed by a changed life and improved behavior. They have undoubtedly (on occasion) afforded a release from pent-up emotions and guilt feelings. In these cases tongues would offer the same therapeutic benefits as losing one's temper and throwing dishes, shouting, or weeping uncontrollably. Also, it seems apparent that tongues, though not caused by the Spirit, can occur in association with a genuine devotional experience. But in any case it is not the tongues speaking which improves the life. The change may be the result of a genuine commitment to God, or more often it may be explainable simply on the psychological level as "turning over a new leaf," a renovation of one's life to make it accord with the new status this experience is mistakenly taken to signify. Even cultists may be changed by their false beliefs and exhibit exemplary and admirable qualities.

The fact that tongues are explainable as a psychological phenomenon and that some psychologists grant that tongues "may be a therapeutic experience in that it releases hidden frustrations and pent-up emotions" (Bloesch, p. 373) should not lead one to conclude that they should be passed off as merely a harmless psychic experience. Even those who speak of their possible benefit hasten to add that this is a dangerous "medicine" and that many "have been psychically damaged by this phenomenon" (Bloesch, p. 373; also Kelsey, p. 227). Bergsma has compared the effects of tongues with the effects of the drug LSD (p. 17). Kelsey has pointed out that some who speak in tongues "have been so overwhelmed by the experience that they never again regained psychological equilibrium" (pp. 206-07). He explains that a person with a weak ego may be so overwhelmed that "the result can be a break with reality and a psychotic state" (p. 207).

There is some evidence that tongues have unusual appeal for those with such "weak egos" and psychological inadequacies. On the basis of their psychological testing, Kildahl and Qualben concluded that "anxiety is a prerequisite for developing the ability to speak in tongues" (Kildahl, p. 58). "Anxiety-free individuals were less apt to seek this kind of experience, . . ." and "persons with a low level of emotional stability tended to be extreme in their affirmation of the benefits of glossolalia" (pp. 58-59). This last statement is particularly interesting in view of the fact that several recent psychological testing programs have been unable to pinpoint specific personality problems as characteristic of tongues speakers. Several studies have intimated, however, that "persons with a low level of emotional stability tended to be extreme in their affirmation of the benefits of glossolalia" and "the more integrated the personality, the more modest" are the tongues speaker's claims regarding the significance of tongues (Kildahl, pp. 59-60). Susan Gilmore concluded that "the open or non-dogmatic Pentecostal believers appear as well-adjusted and interpersonally skillful as do people in general" (p. 164).

There are, however, psychological dangers. In addition, those who are inclined to think of tongues as possibly beneficial should also be reminded of the grave moral and spiritual dangers. The moral dangers may be attested by anyone who has had more than a cursory contact with tongues groups. There seems to be something about the experience of deliberately attempting to throw the conscious mind "out of gear," or perhaps even more important, the emphasis upon "feelings" and sensory perception, which often leads to immorality. Obviously this is not a normal result, but the literature on tongues has well substantiated this possibility. The author has often counseled Christians who, because of the immorality and behavior of tongues-speaking relatives, have concluded that their loved ones are demon possessed. Stegall, Mackie, Stolee and others have cited examples of the vilest of crimes, including murder, committed by those who even at the moment were being "baptized" or seeking the "baptism."

Undoubtedly, the greatest danger associated with tongues lies in the area of the spiritual. Those who have investigated this subject are well aware that tongues often lead to unusual psychic and occult involvement. Spiritual pride, too, often results from the conviction that one is being used miraculously by God. Even sinful actions can be "justified" in the mind of one who believes that God speaks directly to him.

Kildahl and Qualben inferred from their testing that the divisiveness resulting from tongues frequently generates anger and frustration within the tongues speakers. While they generally manifest love toward members of their group, they often exhibit a subtle disrespect for those who do not speak in tongues or do not share their views. This anger or ill will is often projected or vented in prayers which catalog the faults of those who disagree with them. In fact, Kildahl concluded that the spirit of love and unity (group camaraderie) among tongues speakers is dependent upon the recognition that they have a "common enemy," the "out-group" composed of those who do not accept tongues as a genuine work of the Spirit (pp. 68-71).

The greatest spiritual danger, of course, concerns the fact that tongues speakers interpret a purely psychological experience as one of the highest of spiritual achievements, or indeed, even as a divine miracle. The experience is often viewed as a short cut to spirituality and sometimes even accepted as a divine approval of the beliefs and behavior of the speaker.

The view that tongues result from a crisis experience and provide a "psychic catharsis" certainly cannot serve as a causal explanation for most modern tongues, since they are only occasionally associated with a genuine crisis experience. If tongues should occur spontaneously, one might conceive of them as providing some emotional release. But it is difficult to conceive of tongues that result from intensive seeking, coaching, and striving as providing a release from anything other than the pressures of desiring and seeking such an experience. In addition, even if there should be demonstrable evidence that tongues are psychologically beneficial, the dangers, particularly the dangers associated with the misinterpretations of the experience, would far outweigh the benefits.

"Collective psyche."—Based upon the theories of the famous Swiss psychiatrist, Carl Jung, many psychiatrists now view tongues as a manifestation of the "collective unconscious," "universal unconscious," or "collective psyche" as it is variously termed. Kelsey is the most vocal contender for this theory. "If the Jungian idea of the collective unconscious is accepted, speaking in tongues makes real sense, as a breakthrough into consciousness of a deep level of the collective unconscious similar to the dream. Linguistic patterns belonging to the past, to some other part of the present, or to some other level of being take possession of the individual and are expressed by him" (pp. 216-17). Kelsey referred to a meeting where all twelve of the psychiatrists and psychologists present agreed that tongues are a genuine manifestation of this collective unconscious, though some believed that they are of no value, and all apparently felt that there are grave dangers involved (p. 200). In this theory, tongues serve as a sort of "shock therapy" which releases one from his inhibitions and frees him to develop new patterns (p. 201).

Apparently this view is an attempted explanation based upon a misunderstanding of the nature of tongues. It attempts to explain "linguistic patterns" where none exist—at least none of the type contemplated, such as are found in normal languages. It has been ably demonstrated that though tongues speech is not wholly "random," since the syllables are "selected" by the mind on a phonological basis (only), the sounds are lexically and semantically meaningless (Samarin, p. 126). Thus it is unnecessary to seek for an explanation of supposed "linguistic patterns."

The idea of a collective psyche is, moreover, to say the least, only a theory. And it is a theory which cannot be supported by Scripture. Even if psychiatrists should prove that some type of subconscious psychic contact between individuals is possible, this would not prove the existence of a universal or collective unconscious. Bloesch has aptly remarked that attempting to explain tongues by the idea of the collective unconscious "is like trying to explain a riddle by a myth" (p. 372).

Memory excitation.—Both theologians and psychiatrists have often demonstrated that in various types of ecstatic experiences an excitation or exaltation of the memory may occur. In order to show the possible relation of this concept to tongues, it is necessary to (1) be aware of the unusual powers latent in the human mind; (2) cite examples of excited memory; (3) consider the possibility that excited memory may have been involved in the tongues at Pentecost; (4) note that the concept of excited memory could possibly explain certain reports about obscenities occurring in tongues; and (5) consider the possibility that excited memory may have been involved in the tongues at Corinth.

As mentioned in Chapter 1, it has occasionally been reported that foreign languages have occurred in tongues speeches. The author is unaware of any instance where a Christian tongues speech has been recorded and identified as a discourse in a foreign language. Nevertheless, Bloesch has stated that tongues "may even involve the speaking of foreign words, but always words with which the speaker has some if only cursory contact" (p. 372). The human brain has often been compared to a tape recorder or a computer. Nothing can come out except what has been put in. (Obviously, humans may be "inventive," but this involves a correlation of "inputs.") What comes out may be altered, confused, and distorted, but whatever comes out in a tongues speech must, according to this concept, have been introduced sometime in that person's life. Bergsma emphasizes, "Even if that person was not conscious he or she had heard those words, or that a memory engram was being recorded, these had nevertheless been previously deposited there." One could no more speak a language he had never heard, he adds, than he could come from Greece if he had never been there! "It is anatomically, physiologically and psychologically impossible. It is contrary to the laws of the universe. The only exception would be in cases in which God was interposing by means of the miraculous. Present day glossolalists who would claim such repetitious miraculous intervention through their minds day after day, with such insignificant revelations as are being produced today are, it would seem, misguided or are presumptuous. It is like the Himalayan Mountain in obstetrical labor and producing a mouse!" (p. 13).

Baxter, himself a tongues speaker and a "prophet," demonstrated that some of the Irvingite prophecies were elaborations on forgotten newspaper articles. He concluded, "I thus see how things may come into the mind and remain there, and then come forth as supernatural utterances, although their origin was quite natural"

(Mackie, p. 184). Noah Porter stated, "It is questioned by many whether absolute forgetfulness is possible" (Hayes, p. 56). Under the right impulse or circumstances it is conceivable that any thing seen, heard, or experienced may be recalled. Plumptre has shown that those things which have been registered in the brain and cannot be recalled on the conscious level may be recalled during periods of unusual dissociation, such as in fever, ecstasy or trance (Hackett, IV, 3311).

Such a phenomenon could serve as an explanation for most, if not all, of the foreign language elements that have reportedly appeared in tongues. Tongues as they occur among practiced tongues speakers in the modern "charismatic revival" are nearly always consciously induced and are not normally associated with a trance state or unusual dissociation. This could explain why no *recorded* tongues speech has included any clear foreign language elements. Spontaneous tongues, or tongues that appear in association with some crisis or ecstatic experience, might occasionally be expected to contain such elements. Certainly where there is no exceptional emotion or "excitement," one would expect little or no excitation of the memory.

Hayes related two striking examples of such exaltation of the powers of memory. The first of these is from the *Biographia Literaria* of Samuel Taylor Coleridge. He describes a "servant-girl who could neither read nor write, but when seized with a nervous fever, in her delirium talked continuously in Latin and Greek and Hebrew in pompous tones and with most distinct enunciation. Sheets of her ravings were taken down from her mouth, and she was found to be reciting long passages from classical and rabbinical writers. All who heard her were astonished, and many were disposed to believe that she was possessed by a good or an evil spirit. Inquiries were made into the history of her life, and it was learned that, several years before, she had been a servant in the family of an old and learned Protestant pastor in the country, and that pastor had been in the habit of walking up and down a passage of the house adjoining the kitchen and reading aloud to himself favorite portions from the very volumes from which the delirious girl was found to be quoting. She had heard them through the partition. They were utterly unintelligible to her, but these strange sounds had all-unconsciously impressed themselves upon her memory, and in the mental and nervous excitement of her delirium she was able so strangely to recall them and utter them. Under extraordinary mental stimulus such lingual recollections and reproductions are possible" (pp. 58-59). The other example reported by Hayes concerns a Rev. Timothy Flint, who "in his 'Recollections,' records of himself that, when prostrated by malarial fever, he repeated aloud long passages from Virgil and Homer which he had never formally committed to memory, and of which, both before and after his illness, he could repeat scarcely a line" (p. 59).

Though a Christian should insist that the tongues at Pentecost were directly *caused* by the Holy Spirit, without detracting from this fact, the words in the various foreign languages may *possibly* be explained in just such a fashion. Certainly the Spirit *could* have miraculously caused the disciples to deliver clear and logical lectures in unlearned foreign languages, but, as suggested in Chapter 2, the passage itself seems to indicate that this was not the case.

Plumptre has explained that the causes of memory exaltation may be ecstasy, disease, fixed concentration on one object, or an intense sympathy with others who have already entered the abnormal state. He suggests that the Holy Spirit, on the day of Pentecost, may have used this state as His instrument rather than introducing a miracle in all respects without parallel.

With due deference he added, "Questions as to the mode of operation of a power above the common laws of bodily or mental life lead us to a region where our words should be 'wary and few.' There is the risk of seeming to reduce to the known order of nature that which is by confession above and beyond it. In this and in other cases, however, it may be possible, without irreverence or doubt—following the guidance which Scripture itself gives us—to trace in what way the new power did its work, and brought about such wonderful results. It must be remembered, then, that in all likelihood such words as they then uttered had been heard by the disciples before. At every feast which they had ever attended from their youth up, they must have been brought into contact with a crowd as varied as that which was present on the day of Pentecost, the pilgrims of each nation uttering their praises and doxologies. The difference was, that, before, the Galilean peasants had stood in that crowd, neither heeding, nor understanding, nor remembering what they heard, still less able to reproduce it; now they had the power of speaking it clearly and freely. The divine work would in this case take the form of a supernatural exaltation of the memory, not of imparting a miraculous knowledge of words never heard before. We have the authority of John xiv. 26 for seeing in such an exaltation one of the special works of the Divine Comforter" (Hackett, IV, 3309).

Numerous writers have concluded that foreign language elements in tongues, whether in the Spirit-induced variety as at Pentecost or in the humanly produced phenomenon, may be thus explained as resulting from exalted memory. According to Hayes, "The foreign languages spoken at Pentecost are explicable to us as due to abnormally quickened memories, reproducing to these

Jews and proselytes phrases and sentences heard from them, and all-unconsciously stored in minds that had no use of them in normal conditions. The gift of tongues is explicable here as everywhere else, as one form of ecstatic expression, possible at any time of great spiritual uplift, and repeated again and again in the history of the Church" (p. 56).

Chase's comments may help clarify the reasons why the disciples could recite the "wonderful works of God" in many languages. "Now there is evidence that the authorities in Palestine sanctioned the use of any language whatever in repeating the *Shema,* the *Eighteen Benedictions,* and the grace at meals. At other feasts, then, the Apostles had heard strangers of the Dispersion reciting these doxologies in the various languages most familiar to them. Now they in turn themselves, seeing before them Jewish worshippers from many countries, with memories supernaturally quickened, recall and rehearse in the different languages the accustomed words of praise" (p. 39).

Again, Hayes' remarks are worth pondering. He was convinced that the disciples could not have repeated these phrases either before or after Pentecost. It was the excitement of Pentecost, following the wind and flames as signs of the Spirit's arrival, he said, which caused the exaltation of memory. "This, then is our understanding of the phenomenon at Pentecost. There was a real speaking of foreign languages there. That was not the whole of the gift of tongues, and we are not disposed to think that it played any considerable part in the total phenomenon. The phrases and sentences from the foreign languages were in all probability *only the flotsam and jetsam on the general current of speech.* They came to the surface occasionally, and they were doubtless repeated again and again. The most of the speaking was unintelligible, and

Luke has passed it by in his account, for it was just like the glossolalia with which the Early Church had become acquainted in other places. But these foreign phrases, spoken by Galileans who were not linguists and clearly understood by the foreigners of many nations, were the remarkable feature of the phenomenon at Pentecost; and it is this remarkable feature which Luke has taken care to record. These foreign sentences were not natural to the Galilean disciples and were not remembered by them afterward. The use of them is explicable by the powers proven to belong to the subliminal consciousness and the abnormally-quickened memory. All the phrases they repeated they must have heard before at some time or another, though they themselves may not have been conscious of that fact. The same phenomenon is frequent in later Church history, and is common enough today" (pp. 60-61).

Such explanations are not an attempt to remove miracles from the Bible. As demonstrated earlier, the Bible itself indicates that tongues were not miraculous. The suggestion that the Pentecostal tongues contained an element not present on any other occasion of tongues, is, however, in order. This was not the foreign phrases themselves, for foreign phrases may have occurred in other tongues utterances. The distinctive element at Pentecost is that on this occasion *alone* is there any warrant for concluding that the Holy Spirit guided the memories of the apostles in the *selection* of those foreign phrases. There were no blasphemous words or trivial remarks, only ascriptions of praise to God.

Curse words, vulgarities, and blasphemous phrases are among the most forceful expressions in any language. Often they are spoken with clinched fists, stamping of feet, gritting teeth, or a voice raised in anger and bitterness. A middle-aged godly pastor who attended a high school where Spanish was a second language recently told the author that about the only Spanish words he could remember were the vulgarities. Even when spoken in a language not understood by the hearer such words would be those most likely to be impressed upon the subconscious (or sometimes conscious) memory.

These factors may well serve to explain such cases as those reported by A. C. Gaebelein, McCrossan, Matthews, and others, where apparently sincere Christians in their tongues speaking have been heard to speak obscenities in Chinese or other languages unknown to them (Bauman, p. 42; McCrossan, p. 33; Matthews, p. 69). These reports have invariably come from metropolitan centers (San Francisco, Toronto, New York) or other areas where the individual would have had adequate opportunity to hear such foreign language expressions. The curses of a Chinese cook, for example, spoken with vehemence, would make no sense to one unfamiliar with that language, but nevertheless could be strongly impressed upon the unconscious memory, only to be recalled in a moment of dissociation. Recently a language teacher reported having heard an apparently sincere Christian tongues speaker recite obscene words in a foreign language.

It is not necessary to resort to demon activity as an explanation for these foreign language elements in tongues. On the other hand, demons might delight in causing them. They certainly have access to one's thoughts and may guide unconscious thoughts. Sometimes, however, foreign elements are quite meaningless; presumably, demons would have no interest in producing these. A report from southern Texas, for example, where there is a large Mexican population, tells of an English-speaking Pentecostal repeating continually in her tongues such words as the Spanish word for "sweet potato." The speaker could easily have overheard the word in a grocery market.

Foreign language terms, even blasphemies, possibly occurred in the tongues at Corinth! No Christian would ever consciously curse his Lord. But it is *possible* that some at Corinth had spoken such blasphemies in their tongues. In introducing the subject of spiritual gifts, Paul told the Corinthians that no one speaking by the Spirit of God says, 'Jesus is anathema,'' or "Cursed be Jesus" (1 Cor. 12:3). Neander suggests that this "is an expression of the fanatical rejection of Christ, such as might occur in moments of devilish excitement in Jews or heathen" (Lange, X, 248). It is easy to imagine that a Corinthian Christian witnessing to a Jew might have elicited just such a response.

Paul's following clause, "and no one can say Jesus is Lord except by the Spirit," is not exactly parallel to the clause being considered. Some have taught that Paul is merely saying that one cannot say and mean "Jesus is accursed" and be a true Christian, and conversely one cannot say "Jesus is Lord" and truly mean it unless he has been regenerated by the Holy Spirit and is a true Christian. While these are both true statements, Paul's first clause undoubtedly implies more. Certainly any Christian would know that a true Christian would not curse Jesus! Such a statement seems entirely unnecessary if this is all that is meant. Why would Paul say, "I give you to understand," or "I make known to you," such an obvious fact?

His first clause says, "No one *speaking* in the Spirit of God *says*. . . ." He did not merely say, "No one *says* by the Spirit of God, 'Jesus is accursed.' " That would have been parallel to the second clause. The use of the verb *laleō* ("speaking") suggests that Paul had in mind the tongues which had become such a problem at Corinth. In their tongues *speaking (laleō)* some had been heard to *say (legō)* real words of blasphemy. The following clause does not contain the verb *laleō* and does not refer to tongues. It merely states that one cannot truly *say (legō)* "Lord Jesus" or "Jesus is Lord" except as a result of the Spirit's work.

Paul's implication in verses 1 to 3 should not be overlooked. "Now concerning spiritual gifts, brethren, I do not want you to be unaware. You know that when you were pagans you were led astray to the dumb idols, however you were led. Therefore I make known to you, that no one speaking by the Spirit of God says, 'Jesus is accursed'; and no one can say 'Jesus is Lord,' except by the Holy Spirit" (NASB).

As pagans, the Corinthians had been subject to the direction of demonic spirits (see also 10:20-23). Paul suggests that they may *still* allow themselves to be led by such spirits, for they can be assured that the Holy Spirit was not responsible for some of their utterances. He did not explicitly say that their blasphemous words had resulted from demonic influence. He only asserted that the Spirit had not caused them and that consequently the Corinthians should be wary of any possibility of being led astray by other spirits.

Regarding the blasphemous utterances mentioned here, Hayes remarked, "Paul repudiated all suggestion of responsibility on the part of the Spirit of God for such expressions, even if they occurred with other pious ones in the speech of the people who were speaking with tongues. The devil might take advantage of one in that experience and make use of the tongues, over which the understanding had no control, just as easily as the Spirit of God" (pp. 50-51).

One thing is quite clear. The Spirit of God is not responsible for any blasphemous utterances, whether in tongues or otherwise.

The concept of excited memory offers a plausible explanation for the occasional reports of foreign language elements in modern tongues. It is also possible to understand this as explaining some aspects of the Biblical phenomenon. Only in the case of the tongues at Pentecost is there warrant for concluding that the Holy Spirit guided the memories of the tongues speakers in ascribing praise to God.

Why the present interest in tongues?

The unsatisfied longing for a genuine religious expression in the midst of the pressures of a secularized society has undoubtedly contributed to the "charismatic revival." Tongues have offered a "release" from this pressure, a means of religious expression which, however, leaves unsatisfied man's deepest longings for spiritual reality. It is easily demonstrable that many persons who have had this experience do not exhibit those characteristics which the New Testament lists as indicative of true spiritual reality (Gal. 5:22-23). It is also noteworthy that those who are most zealous for tongues are nearly always those who were converted to the movement as adults following a period of anxiety or spiritual dissatisfaction (see Kildahl, pp. 57-58). Second-generation Pentecostals seem to have less enthusiasm for the experience and definitely speak in tongues with less frequency than adult converts (see Samarin, pp. 194, 240).

Repression.—Many writers have remarked that tongues movements among Christians have arisen during periods of persecution or declining religious interest. Persecution, deism, and skepticism have been named as specific causes. Hinson has stated that these factors suggest one major reason for the manifestation of tongues: "the restraining or repression of religion," either actively or passively (p. 72). In writing about tongues among the Cevenols, Hayes remarked "It was the sword and bayonet which caused them, rather than caused them to cease" (p. 70). According to Ruble, in some cases tongues have apparently been brought on by emotional stresses (p. 44).

Insecurity.—Psychological surveys and studies have often concluded that as a group tongues speakers "represent varying degrees of personality abnormality" (Jennings, p. 8). Lapsley and Simpson, professors at Princeton Theological Seminary, suggested that tongues represent a truncated personality development (p. 55). Several recent studies, however, have reported that tongues speakers are generally "normally adjusted and productive members of society" (Hine, p. 216; see also Gilmore and Plog). Perhaps this more generous attitude may be largely explained by the recent increase of tongues among the cultured and socially advantaged. Most of these recent tests have concerned neo-Pentecostal groups whose tongues are now approved in many traditional denominations.

But even these favorable assessments, such as one that concludes that tongues speakers "are neither more nor less emotionally disturbed than equally religious non-tongues-speakers," nearly always add a "nevertheless" or some other qualification(s) (Kildahl, p. 65). Such assessments are usually limited to the less zealous or "non-dogmatic" tongues speakers (Gilmore, p. 164), or merely purport to show that "no gross pathology" is necessary for this experience (see Samarin, p. 19). They then go on to posit insecurity, an unusual need for social acceptance, anxiety, dependency, and so forth, as characteristic of tongues speakers. These are obviously not grossly abnormal or serious pathological disorders.

But psychological testing produces varying results depending upon the psychologist's prejudices and the difference in groups of subjects. Nearly all reports do suggest, however, that tongues may have a special appeal for those with personal inadequacies. Based on his testing, one expert concluded that tongues attract "uncertain, threatened, inadequately-organized persons with strong motivation to reach a state of satisfactory interpersonal relatedness and personal integrity" (Wood, pp. 93-96). Another found that tongues speakers tended to come from distrubed home environments and evidenced more insecurity than the control groups who did not speak in tongues. "They are people," he said, "who, psychologically speaking, have had a poor beginning in life. This has been reflected by the difficulty in adjustment to their home situation in infancy and later adulthood" (Vivier, p. 432). Still another reported that "weak egos, confused identities, high levels of anxiety . . . unstable personality . . . chaotic religious backgrounds, and a remarkable degree of emotional deprivation" are evidenced among tongues speakers (see Oates, p. 97).

Spiritual hunger.—It seems to be granted by theologians that the "charismatic revival" represents a deep, unsatisfied religious hunger. Modernistic main-line churches have supplied nothing to satisfy man's spiritual hunger, and too often fundamentalist churches have represented only a dead orthodoxy with little evidence of true spirituality.

In this vein Bloesch remarks: "The deep-seated yearning for sanctification or holiness is also a note that can be appreciated in the neo-Pentecostal revival. This movement cannot be fully understood unless it is seen as a protest against the creeping secularization in main-line Protestantism. Many Protestant churches have focused their attention on their own institutional needs to such extent that they have failed to meet the deeper needs of the spirit. The principal concern of too many churches has been the expansion of the organization rather than the glory of God and the salvation of men. What is lacking among many modern Christians is piety or spirituality" (p. 378).

Even in evangelical and fundamental churches, the "program"—even though it may be a good program—has too often taken precedence over a concern for manifesting the fruit of the Spirit.

A secularized society.—It is not merely coincidental that within the past decade both the "God is dead" theology and the "charismatic revival" came to prominence. The "God is dead" theology is a natural result of the tendencies against which the charismatic revival is a protest. These tendencies include the dominance of "science" and the resulting secularization of society, along with the corollary loss of true piety and a proper concern for the work of the Spirit in the daily life of each believer.

The need for expression.—Due to the repression of true religion, modern man seems to find it increasingly difficult to talk about his own *personal* relationship with God. In this scientific and secularized society many are embarrassed when the name of Jesus enters into a serious conversation or when heaven, hell, or salvation are mentioned. "It is not sex which is a delicate subject in our generation but religion," says McClelland. Undergraduates "talk readily enough about their sex lives," a psychologist reports, "but unwillingly and with great hesitation about their religious convictions" (Oates, p. 79).

According to Wayne Oates, "Mid-century secular society represses and selectively ignores religion in reference to God, except as a joke or as profanity. The easy, spontaneous discussion of religion, particularly in its intimate personal aspects, no longer exists. It takes 'brash-ness,' 'directness,' and even 'compulsiveness' to speak openly of God in many circles today. Even the courage to speak of God directly and personally as nurtured by the neo-evangelicals . . . and by theological institutions has a sort of forced necessity about it. The milieu in which we live has become overwhelmingly inarticulate about God especially in the home, the place where language is learned initially. As Paul M. van Buren has put it, 'Our inherited language of the supernatural has indeed died "the death of a thousand qualifications" ' " (pp. 79-80).

The Bible teaches that man was created in the image of God and that consequently there is an "infinity" in man's heart (Eccles. 3:11) which cannot be satisfied apart from a proper personal relationship with his Creator. In addi-tion, it has been said that "communication is the essence of being human" (Oates, p. 90). This would suggest that man cannot be wholly satisfied apart from a proper re-lationship with his Creator *and* a personal *expression* of that relationship. Yet today few Christian homes provide an atmosphere which fosters discussion of personal spirit-ual concerns. Such discussion has been all but outlawed in public school education. In Oates' opinion, one of the "side effects" of public education is to render young people "inarticulate about their faith at the time of their most intensive study of the language of their native tongue" (p. 80).

The church has offered little help. Informal conversa-tions before and after church services rarely focus on Biblical truth or personal spiritual concerns. The word "fellowship" often designates only refreshments or a con-versation about the weather, the pastor, and clothes.

With religious and spiritual expression so repressed, it it not surprising that an experience which professes to offer a *personal* relationship with God and an avenue for the expression of religious feelings should gain widespread acceptance.

Since society in this age cannot be desecularized, since most churches will remain merely social organizations, and since many Christians will never experience the true joy of walking in the Spirit, the tongues movement will continue until our Lord returns or until it either discredits itself by its excesses or becomes accepted as itself only a formality.

The Christian opportunity.—Many are attracted to the tongues movement because of an unsatisfied longing for a deeper spiritual life. This inmost hunger of man's being can be satisfied when the Spirit of God and the Word of God are given their proper place. Tongues offer a series of isolated experiences as a substitute for a constant expression and awareness of the Spirit. Evangelical Christians should not only attempt to bring persons to Christ, but should also foster opportunities in the home, in Christian schools, and in the church for expression of spiritual concerns, convictions, and aspirations.

It is the opportunity of Christian experience to be continually being conformed to the image of Christ (Rom. 8:29; 2 Cor. 3:18; Col. 3:10) as the Spirit is allowed to produce the characteristics of Christ in the believer (Gal. 5:22). The Spirit does not draw attention to Himself, but to Christ (Jn. 16:14). When the characteristics of Christ are being produced by the fullness of the indwelling Spirit, man's deepest longings for spiritual reality are fully satisfied and find joyous and *meaningful* expression.

CHAPTER 6

Summaries
and
Conclusions

As a result of the preceding study the following summary statements are in order.

The Significance of Modern Tongues

Tongues are not self-authenticating. Tongues speaking occurs among non-Christians as well as among Christians. It occurs in other religions and also even in nonreligious contexts. It occurs among carnal, worldly, and immature Christians as well as among Christians who evidence admirable spiritual qualities. The experience, therefore, cannot be understood as, in itself, a proof of anything except that tongues are a possibility for all kinds of persons regardless of their spiritual condition.

The Purpose of Biblical Tongues

The Holy Spirit's purpose in causing tongues was to authenticate those specially appointed representatives of Christ—the apostles. Tongues speaking was a sign of His presence and ministry for the purpose of validating the apostolic message before it was inscripturated. As a devotional experience it was personally edifying to the speaker. Since it was sometimes a spontaneous expression of devotion (always when it was caused by the Spirit), God sometimes granted the gift of interpretation so that others might also be edified.

The Nature of Biblical Tongues

New Testament tongues should be understood as a nonmiraculous expression of devotion resulting from the work of the Holy Spirit in the believer. The original occurrence of tongues in each case in the Apostolic Age was associated with the ministry of the apostles. Probably the Holy Spirit directly caused only the *first* use of tongues for each individual. But once the believer had spoken in tongues at the compulsion of the Holy Spirit, he was apparently able to exercise the ability whenever he desired. This explains the misuse of a divinely given ability at Corinth.

In all cases where tongues are not merely pretended, both Biblical and modern, they involve an unintelligible extemporaneous speech which, though in some ways phonologically similar to language, is syntactically meaningless. There are occasional reports of foreign language elements being included in these otherwise unintelligible speeches. When authentic, these may point to an exaltation of memory. It is possible that foreign words, phrases, or sentences, forgotten on the conscious level, may be recalled from the subconscious level during this experience. This might be expected only in cases of trance, ecstasy, or unusual excitement. This may have been the case at Pentecost, or the tongues on that occasion may have been uniquely miraculous.

The Duration of Biblical Tongues

The purpose for Biblical tongues obviously limits them to the Apostolic Age. In addition, no matter how one understands "that which is perfect," 1 Corinthians 13 intimates that tongues would cease before the revelatory gifts. This passage does *not* state that tongues were to continue until replaced by "that which is perfect." Even the revelatory gifts, *as far as the Church Age is concerned,* are linked to the foundational stage of the church (Eph. 2:20). Historical evidence also points to a cessation of Spirit-caused tongues within the Apostolic Age.

Paul's prediction, "Tongues . . . shall cease," did not mean that no one would ever speak in tongues after the Apostolic Age. Pagans had spoken in tongues previously and both pagans and Christians have often done so since. Paul simply meant that the Holy Spirit would not initiate tongues. He had done so only for a purpose, and that purpose would no longer exist. Just as self-styled "prophets" have claimed that their messages were from God, so there have been tongues speakers who have claimed that their tongues were caused by God.

The Source of Modern Tongues

On one occasion Jesus asked the chief priests and scribes, "The baptism of John, was it from heaven, or of men?" (Lk. 20:4). We may ask, "The tongues of today, are they from heaven or of men?" We cannot, as the scribes did, refuse to answer. Certainly it is just as evil to attribute to the Holy Spirit that which is *not* His work as to attribute to another what truly *is* the Spirit's work. One who accepts the Scriptures as authoritative should not attribute modern tongues to the Holy Spirit. The Spirit Himself, in His Word, limits His causation of the phenomenon to the Apostolic Age. Though the father of lies (Jn. 8:44) and his demonic agents are active in the propagation of all perversions of true doctrine, the primary explanation for individual tongues utterances is to be found in the psychological constitution of man himself.

The Modern Interest in Tongues

The modern interest in tongues in many cases indicates an unsatisfied spiritual hunger. The attempt to fill such a hunger by indulgence in a psychological experience is analogous to satisfying physical hunger by drinking water. The stomach can be filled with water, but without real food, eventually starvation is certain.

The success of modern glossolalia is explainable by three primary factors: (1) the hunger for a truly personal religious experience and for a personal *expression* of such experience; (2) the social pressures bearing upon one who has been led to believe, or whose peers believe, that this experience is necessary for spiritual' reality; and (3) the narcissistic rewards which are gained by such a supposedly obvious expression of divine favor.

Concluding Observations

In closing this study it is fitting to remark upon (1) Paul's injunction against forbidding tongues speaking, (2) the wholesome aspects of Pentecostalism, and (3) the Christian's responsibility in this age.

Paul's injunction against forbidding tongues

Frequently Paul's caution, "Forbid not to speak in tongues," is given in response to any argument against tongues. These words, however, were written in A.D. 55 to a group of people who had originally received the ability under the direct causation of the Holy Spirit in accordance with its divine purpose. The Holy Spirit had not yet ceased causing the gift, since the ministry of the apostles was still being authenticated by signs. Also, even though Paul wrote to people who had been given the gift of tongues by the Holy Spirit, he himself gave restrictions which strictly limited the use of the gift. One should not forget that Paul also predicted the cessation of the gift.

In addition, note that technically the point to which we object is not the *fact* of tongues speaking, but the *reasons* which lead one to seek this experience and the *interpretations of its significance.* Since tongues are merely a psychological phenomenon, it is *conceivable* that one could speak in tongues simply as the result of some overpowering emotion without deliberately seeking this experience for some supposed spiritual benefit. Especially in some cultures would this seem feasible, though it is doubtful that tongues would occur in the United States apart from either a conscious or unconscious desire for the experience. Furthermore, we have seen that tongues may result from fever or some other illness involving dissociation. To label such a psychological experience under such circumstances as "evil" would be as pointless as labeling uncontrollable weeping or dreaming as evil.

Consequently, tongues speaking is not, in itself, morally evil—though it should be recognized as potentially dangerous. It *is* evil to seek tongues as necessary for certain spiritual benefits, to consider them as proof of certain spiritual blessings, or to label them as caused by the Holy Spirit, for to do so is to contradict not only the facts of history and psychology, but also Scriptural revelation.

Many books and articles on the subject of tongues have been published in recent years. All writers who have approached the subject objectively (those outside the movement and even several within it) have concluded that contemporary tongues are not miraculous. Without denying the real possibility of demonic influence, speaking in tongues is viewed as normally a psychological experience in which thousands of persons have engaged without serious detriment to their well-being, and many have even reported that they have been positively benefited.

For this reason many writers conclude with a sympathetic evaluation of the experience. "Normally," they say, "tongues speakers are confused as to what tongues are, and why they should be sought. The important thing is, they think they are helped and this is all that matters!" Or, it may be concluded, tongues may be viewed as legitimate and of value because, after all, "the mystery of religion is symbolized" as in the eucharist, and they do serve to mark "the discontinuity between the sacred and the profane" Samarin, pp. 232-33).

Evangelical Christians should object to these conclusions. One may be sympathetic toward tongues speakers without being sympathetic toward the experience and the movement. One should not approve false interpretations of the eucharist (like transubstantiation), for example, merely because the mystery of religion is symbolized. Likewise, one should not approve of snake-handling, though its practitioners certainly view it as marking the discontinuity between the sacred and the profane.

To argue that tongues speaking should be approved, in spite of misinterpretations of its cause and nature, because its practitioners profess to be benefited, is like arguing that cultist doctrines should be approved because the cultists have been favorably changed by their beliefs.

Wholesome aspects of Pentecostalism

Pentecostalism has some admirable aspects. Its emphasis upon a personal religious experience is certainly commendable, especially in contrast to the societal emphasis in main-line denominations. Its interest in eschatology is wholesome, though unfortunately not many Pentecostals or even neo-Pentecostals have been scholarly or Biblical in their exegesis. Congregational singing is hearty. This is a legitimate avenue of religious expression which has too often been displaced by choirs or by what amounts to a mere moving of lips in unison. And the informality of Pentecostal services is, in many ways, preferable to the staid formalism of many church services.

The Christian's responsibility

What is needed today is a Biblically correct emphasis on a personal relationship with the triune God. Man *must* be rightly related to God and must be able to *express* himself concerning this relationship. Two doctrines must be specially emphasized: (1) the necessity for a conversion experience through personal acceptance of Jesus as Saviour, and (2) the responsibility of the believer to be rightly related to the indwelling Holy Spirit so as to allow the true fruits of His presence to develop. A proper emphasis on the Spirit's ministry in the life of the believer is essential. As Paul tells us in Galatians 5:22-23, "The fruit of the Spirit is love, joy, peace, longsuffering, gentleness, goodness, faithfulness, meekness, self-control . . ."—not tongues.

Bibliography of Works Cited

Abbott-Smith, G. *A Manual Greek Lexicon of the New Testament.* Edinburgh: T. & T. Clark, 1954.

Alford, Henry. *The Greek Testament.* 4 vols. 6th ed. London: Rivingtons, 1871.

Arndt, William F., and Gingrich, F. Wilbur. *A Greek-English Lexicon of the New Testament.* Chicago: University of Chicago Press, 1957.

Augustine. "On Baptism, Against the Donatists." Translated by J. R. King. *The Nicene and Post-Nicene Fathers*, edited by Philip Schaff, vol. 4, first series. Buffalo, N. Y.: Christian Literature Co. 1887.

_____. "Ten Homilies on the First Epistle of John." Translated by H. Browne. *The Nicene and Post-Nicene Fathers*, edited by Philip Schaff, vol. 7, first series. New York: Christian Literature Co., 1888.

Bach, Marcus. *The Inner Ecstasy.* New York: World Publishing Co., 1969.

Barnes, Albert. *Barnes' Notes on the New Testament.* Grand Rapids: Kregel Publications, 1966.

Bauman, Louis S. *The Tongues Movement.* Winona Lake, Ind.: Brethren Missionary Herald Co., 1963.

Bell, Henry. "Speaking in Tongues." Th.D. dissertation, Dallas Theological Seminary, 1930.

Bellshaw, William G. "The Confusion of Tongues." *Bibliotheca Sacra* 120 (April-June 1963): pp. 145-53.

Bergsma, Stuart. *Speaking with Tongues.* Grand Rapids: Baker Book House, 1965.

Bloesch, Donald G. "The Charismatic Revival." *Religion in Life,* summer 1966, pp. 364-80.

Boyer, James L. *For a World Like Ours: Studies in I Corinthians.* Winona Lake, Ind.: BMH Books, 1971.

Brown, Francis; Driver, S. R.; and Briggs, Charles A. *A Hebrew and English Lexicon of the Old Testament.* Based on the lexicon of William Gesenius as translated by Edward Robinson. Oxford: Clarendon Press, 1959.

Brumback, Carl. *What Meaneth This?* Springfield, Mo.: Gospel Publishing House, 1961.

Burdick, Donald W. *Tongues: To Speak or Not to Speak.* Chicago: Moody Press, 1969.

Cawood, John. *The New Tongues Movement.* Philadelphia: Philadelphia College of Bible, n. d.

Chase, Frederick Henry. *The Credibility of the Book of the Acts of the Apostles.* London: Macmillan and Co., 1902.

Christenson, Laurence. *Speaking in Tongues.* Minneapolis: Bethany Fellowship Publishers, 1968.

Chrysostom. "Homilies on First Corinthians." Translated by T. W. Chambers. *The Nicene and Post-Nicene Fathers,* edited by Philip Schaff, vol. 12, first series. New York: Christian Literature Co., 1889.

Cutten, George B. *Speaking with Tongues: Historically and Psychologically Considered.* New Haven, Conn.: Yale University Press, 1927.

Dake, Finis Jennings. *Dake's Annotated Reference Bible.* Atlanta: Dake Bible Sales, 1963.

Dalton, Robert Chandler. *Tongues Like as of Fire.* Springfield, Mo.: Gospel Publishing House, 1945.

Dana, H. E., and Mantey, Julius R. *A Manual Grammar of the Greek New Testament.* New York: Macmillan Co., 1953.

Dungey, John William. "The Relationship of *Pauō* in 1 Corinthians 13:8 to the Modern Tongues Movement." Th.M. thesis, Dallas Theological Seminary, 1967.

Ervin, Howard M. *These Are Not Drunken, as Ye Suppose.* Plainfield, N. J.: Logos International, 1968.

Farrell, Frank. "Outburst of Tongues: The New Penetration." *Christianity Today* (a collection of articles from *Christianity Today*), edited by Frank E. Gaebelein. Westwood, N. J.: Fleming H. Revell Co., 1966.

Gee, Donald. *Speaking in Tongues—The Initial Evidence of the Baptism in the Holy Spirit.* Toronto: Full Gospel Publishing House, n. d.

Gesenius, William. *Gesenius' Hebrew and Chaldee Lexicon.* Translated by Samuel Prideaux Tregelles. Grand Rapids: Wm. B. Eerdmans Publishing Co., 1964.

Gilmore, Susan K. "Personality Differences Between High and Low Dogmatism Groups of Pentecostal Believers." *Journal for the Scientific Study of Religion* 8 (1969), pp. 161-64.

Godet, Frederick L. *Commentary on the First Epistle of St. Paul to the Corinthians.* 2 vols. Translated by A. Cusin. Grand Rapids: Zondervan Publishing House, 1957.

Gromacki, Robert Glenn. *The Modern Tongues Movement.* Philadelphia: Presbyterian and Reformed Publishing Co., 1967.

Hackett, H. B., ed. *Smith's Dictionary of the Bible.* 4 vols. New York: Hurd and Houghton, 1871.

Harris, Laird. *Inspiration and Canonicity of the Bible.* Grand Rapids: Zondervan Publishing House, 1957.

Hayes, D. A. *The Gift of Tongues.* New York: Methodist Book Concern, 1913.

Hine, Virginia H. "Non-pathological Pentecostal Glossolalia: A Summary of Relevant Psychological Literature." *Journal for the Scientific Study of Religion* 8 (1964), pp. 211-26.

Hinson, E. Glenn. "A Brief History of Glossolalia." In Stagg [see below], Hinson and Oates. *Glossolalia.* Nashville: Abingdon Press, 1967.

Hitt, Russell T. "The New Pentecostalism." Reprinted from *Eternity,* July 1963, pp. 1-8.

Hodge Charles. *An Exposition of the First Epistle to the Corinthians.* Grand Rapids: Wm. B. Eerdmans Publishing Co., 1950.

Hoekema, Anthony A. *What About Tongue-Speaking?* Grand Rapids: Wm. B. Eerdmans Publishing Co., 1966.

Horton, Harold. *What Is the Good of Speaking with Tongues?* London: Assemblies of God Publishing House, 1960.

Hutchins, R. M., ed. *Great Books of the Western World.* Vols. 7, 13. Chicago: Encyclopedia Britannica, 1952.

Jennings, George J. "An Ethnological Study of Glossolalia." *Journal of the American Scientific Affiliation* 20 (March 1, 1968), pp. 5-16.

Kelsey, Morton T. *Tongue Speaking.* Garden City, N. Y.: Double-day and Co., 1964.

Kendrick, Klaude. *The Promise Fulfilled.* Springfield, Mo.: Gospel Publishing House, 1961.

Kildahl, John P. *The Psychology of Speaking in Tongues.* New York: Harper and Row, Publishers, 1972.

Kittel, Gerhard, ed. *Theological Dictionary of the New Testament.* Translated and edited by Geoffrey Bromiley. Vols. 1-5, edited by Gerhard Kittel; vol. 6, edited by Gerhard Friedrich. Grand Rapids: Wm. B. Eerdmans Publishing Co., 1964-72.

Kling, Christian Friedrich. "The First Epistle of Paul to the Corinthians." Translated by David W. Poor, vol. 10, *Lange's Commentary on the Holy Scriptures.* Edited by Philip Schaff. Grand Rapids: Zondervan Publishing House, 1960.

Lange, John Peter, ed. *Lange's Commentary on the Holy Scriptures.* 12 vols. Edited by Philip Schaff. Grand Rapids: Zondervan Publishing House, 1960.

Lapsley, James N. and J. H. Simpson. "Speaking in Tongues: Token of Group Acceptance and Divine Approval." *Pastoral Psychology* 144 (May 1964), pp. 48-55. "Speaking in Tongues: Infantile Babble or Song of the Self?" *Pastoral Psychology* 146 (September 1964), pp. 16-24.

Lenski, R. C. H. *The Interpretations of St. Paul's First and Second Epistles to the Corinthians.* Columbus, Ohio: Wartburg Press, 1946.

Liddell, Henry George, and Scott, Robert. 9th ed. Revised by Henry Stuart Jones. *A Greek-English Lexicon.* Oxford University Press, 1953.

Lightner, Robert P. *Speaking in Tongues and Divine Healing.* Des Plaines, Ill.: Regular Baptist Press, 1965.

Mackie, Alexander. *The Gift of Tongues.* New York: George H. Doran Co., 1921.

Martin, Ira Jay. *Glossolalia in the Apostolic Church.* Berea, Ky.: Berea College Press, 1960.

Matthews, John. *Speaking in Tongues.* Kansas City, Mo.: John Matthews, 1925.

McCrossan, T. J. *Speaking with Other Tongues.* Harrisburg, Pa.:

Christian Alliance Publishing Co., n. d.

Meyer, Heinrich August Wilhelm. *Critical and Exegetical Handbook of the Epistles to the Corinthians,* vol. 2, translated by D. Douglas Bannerman. *Critical and Exegetical Commentary on the New Testament.* 17 vols., edited by William P. Dickson and William Stewart. Edinburgh: T. & T. Clark, 1884.

Mills, Watson E. *Understanding Speaking in Tongues.* William B. Eerdmans Publishing Co., 1972.

Moulton, James Hope, and Milligan, George. *The Vocabulary of the Greek New Testament.* London: Hodder and Stoughton, 1929.

New American Standard Bible (Cited as NASB). La Habra, Calif.: Foundation Press Publications, publisher for the Lockman Foundation, 1971.

Northrup, Bernard E. "Tongues and Temporary Gifts." Unpublished research paper, San Francisco Conservative Baptist Theological Seminary, n. d.

Oates, Wayne E. "A Socio-Psychological Study of Glossolalia." In Stagg [see below], Hinson, and Oates. *Glossolalia.* Nashville: Abingdon Press. 1967.

Orr, James, ed. *The International Standard Bible Encyclopedia.* 5 vols. Grand Rapids: Wm. B. Eerdmans Publishing Co. 1939.

Plog, Stanley C. "UCLA Conducts Research on Glossolalia." Trinity Whitsuntide. 1964, pp. 38-39.

Pritchard, James R., ed. *Ancient Near Eastern Texts.* Princeton, N. J.: Princeton University Press, 1950.

Rice, John R. *Speaking with Tongues.* Wheaton, Ill.: Sword of the Lord Publications, 1963.

Roberts, Alexander, and Donaldson, James. *The Ante-Nicene Fathers.* 10 vols. Grand Rapids: Wm. B. Eerdmans Publishing Co., 1950.

Rogers, Cleon L., Jr. "The Gift of Tongues in the Post Apostolic Church." *Bibliotheca Sacra* 122 (April-June 1965): pp. 134-143.

Ruble, Richard Lee. "A Scriptural Evaluation of Tongues in Contemporary Theology." Th.D. dissertation, Dallas Theological Seminary, 1964.

Samarin, William J. *Tongues of Men and Angels.* New York: Macmillan Co., 1972.

Schaff, Philip. *History of the Christian Church.* 8 vols. Grand Rapids: Wm. B. Eerdmans Publishing Co., 1951.

Scroggie, W. Graham. *The Baptism of the Holy Spirit and Speaking with Tongues.* London: Pickering and Inglis, n. d.

_____. *Speaking with Tongues.* New York: Book Stall, 1919.

Sherrill, John L. *They Speak with Other Tongues.* Westwood, N. J.: Fleming H. Revell, 1964.

Staats, C. Gary. Personal correspondence with author. October 31, 1972.

Stagg, Frank; Hinson, E. Glenn; and Oates, Wayne E. *Glossolalia: Tongue Speaking in Biblical, Historical, and Psychological Perspective.* Nashville, Tenn.: Abingdon Press, 1967.

Stegall, Carroll, Jr. *The Modern Tongues and Healing Movement.* Shalimar, Fla.: Carroll Stegall, n. d.

Stolee, H. J. *Speaking in Tongues.* Minneapolis: Augsburg Publishing House, 1963.

Trench, Richard Chenevix. *Synonyms of the New Testament.* Grand Rapids: Wm. B. Eerdmans Publishing Co., 1953.

Unger, Merrill F. *New Testament Teaching on Tongues.* Grand Rapids: Kregel Publications, 1971.

Vivier, L. M. Van Eetveldt. "Glossolalia." Dissertation for Doctor of Medicine in the Department of Psychiatry and Mental Hygiene. University of Witwatersand, Iohannesburg, South Africa, 1960. [Available on microfilm at the University of Chicago Library, Chicago.]

Walvoord, John F. *The Holy Spirit.* 3rd ed. Findlay, Ohio: Dunham Publishing Co., 1958.

Warfield, Benjamin B. *Miracles: Yesterday and Today, True and False.* Grand Rapids: Wm. B. Eerdmans Publishing Co., 1965.

Whitcomb, John C., *Does God Want Christians To Perform Miracles Today?* Winona Lake, Indiana: BMH Books, 1973.

Wood, William W. *Culture and Personality Aspects of the Pentecostal Holiness Religion.* The Hague: Mouton and Co., 1965.